Alexa

First Architect of the American Government

By Michael W. Simmons

Table of Contents

Introduction

"In no part of the constitution is more wisdom to be found than in the clause which confides the question of war or peace to the legislature, and not to the executive department. Beside the objection to such a mixture of heterogeneous powers: the trust and the temptation would be too great for any one man: not such as nature may offer as the prodigy of many centuries, but such as may be expected in the ordinary successions of magistracy. War is in fact the true nurse of executive aggrandizement. In war a physical force is to be created, and it is the executive will which is to direct it. In war the public treasures are to be unlocked, and it is the executive hand which is to dispense them. In war the honors and emoluments of office are to be multiplied; and it is the executive patronage under which they are to be enjoyed. It is in war, finally, that laurels are to be gathered, and it is the executive brow they are to encircle. The strongest passions, and most dangerous weaknesses of the human breast; ambition, avarice, vanity, the honorable or venial love of fame, are all in conspiracy against the desire and duty of peace."

Alexander Hamilton, 1794

America's "founding fathers" are amongst the most closely studied individuals in modern history. Their lineage, parentage, education, and early careers have been exhaustively documented and studied, and their origin stories are part of this nation's national mythology. From Washington and Jefferson's antecedents as privileged Virginia planters, to Adams's ambitious transformation from the son of a shoemaker to Massachusetts lawyer, scholars have preserved the details of their biographies in as much detail as the records of the battles they fought and the political victories that defined their presidencies.

Alexander Hamilton and the other men who brought the United States of America into being were deeply sensible of the uniqueness of their historical position. Never before in European history had citizens wrested a colony from the hands of a king and created a self-governing republic. The founders were legends in their own lifetimes, and, conscious of the fact that their lives would be studied, they took an active role in shaping their own legacies, by telling their stories as they wished them to be remembered.

None of the founding fathers were more anxious for their legacies than Alexander Hamilton. He was extraordinarily ambitious even by the standards of his peers in the early republic. However, until fairly recently, he has been amongst the most obscure figures from America's first decades. Though he was the nation's first treasury secretary, and was the most powerful figure in Washington's first cabinet after Washington himself, his enormous accomplishments have been comparatively forgotten—due perhaps to the fact that he died comparatively young, while his political enemies lived on to write their own versions of his history.

Hamilton's obscurity is undeserved, however; the astounding scope of his learning and accomplishments, combined with the personal hardships he overcame to achieve his place in history, make him a riveting figure for study. Contemporary readers are in a better place to appreciate just how much he achieved than Hamilton's own contemporaries, having access to details about his early life that Hamilton concealed during his lifetime. As an immigrant in the 18th century, Hamilton suffered much of the same stigma faced by immigrants in the 21st century. In order to be regarded as the equal of men like Washington and Jefferson, Hamilton felt the need to conceal and downplay his origins as much as possible; some of his more snobbish colleagues, like John Adams, took shots at his West Indian upbringing and illegitimate birth whenever they clashed with him politically, unaware that in so doing they were placing themselves on the wrong side of history.

To most students in the 21st century, Alexander Hamilton's humble beginnings are relatable in a way that the aristocratic antecedents of most of his colleagues are not. His background makes him not only more interesting, but arguably more admirable than other founders who had to work less hard and still achieved less. Hamilton was, in many ways, the original embodiment of the American dream, the nation's first truly self-made man, an immigrant who came to the new world as a teenager to better his condition in life and join the struggle for independence. Many Americans have walked in his footsteps since then, but none have played so extraordinary a role in shaping the government of a new nation.

Chapter One: The West Indies

Rachel Faucette and James Hamilton

"The truth is that on the question who my parents were, I have better pretensions than most of those who in this Country plume themselves on Ancestry.

"My Grandfather by the mothers side of the name of Faucette was a French Huguenot who emigrated to the West Indies in consequence of the revocation of the Edict of Nantz and settled in the Island of Nevis and there acquired a pretty fortune. I have been assured by persons who knew him that he was a man of letters and much of a gentleman. He practiced as a Physician, whether that was his original profession, or one assumed for livelihood after his emigration is not to me ascertained.

"My father now dead was certainly of a respectable Scotch Family. His father was, and the son of his Eldest brother now is Laird of Grange. His mother was the sister of an ancient Baronet Sir Robert Pollock.

"Himself being a younger son of a numerous family was bred to trade. In capacity of merchant he went to St Kitts, where from too generous and too easy a temper he failed in business, and at length fell into indigent circumstances. For some time he was supported by his friends in Scotland, and for several years before his death by me. It was his fault to have had too much pride and two large a portion of indolence—but his character was otherwise without reproach and his manners those of a Gentleman.

"So far I may well challenge comparison, but the blemish remains to be unveiled.

"A Dane - a fortune-hunter of the name of Lavine - came to Nevis bedizzened with gold, and paid his addresses to my mother then a handsome young woman having a snug fortune. In compliance with the wishes of her mother who was captivated by the glitter of the --, but against her own inclination she married Lavine. The marriage was unhappy and ended in a separation by divorce. My mother afterwards went to St Kitts, became acquainted with my father and a marriage between them ensued, followed by many years cohabitation and several children.

"But unluckily it turned out that the divorce was not absolute but qualified, and thence the second marriage was not lawful. Hence when my mother died the small property which she left went to my half brother Mr Lavine who lived in South Carolina and was for a time partner with Mr Kane. He is now dead."

Letter from Alexander Hamilton to William Jackson, August of 1800, containing the only description of his family background that he ever committed to paper.

About the earliest years of Alexander Hamilton's life, little is known for certain outside of the details he himself provides in the above letter to William Jackson, which Hamilton wrote after President John Adams accused him of being a bastard in front of a member of his cabinet. The uncertainty extends to the precise date of Hamilton's birth.

After journeying to America to attend college, Hamilton gave his birthdate as January 11, 1757; there is, however, evidence in the form of court documents to suggest that he was actually born in 1755. It was not unheard of, in past centuries when record keeping was less uniform, for people to be uncertain of their birth date or year, but Hamilton probably knew the date and deliberately concealed it to make himself appear younger than he was. Having come to America to attend university, Hamilton was older than most of his fellow students—in the 1700s it was customary to attend colleague at the age of about 14 or 15—and it no doubt seemed less embarrassing to be thought of as only two years behind his classmates, rather than four or five.

Hamilton was absurdly precocious as a child, and if he had been born in the American colonies, with easy access to a regular education, he may well have been like his lifelong rival Aaron Burr, who began his collegiate studies at the age of 11. But when Hamilton was an adolescent, his genius was entirely consumed by the task of surviving as an orphan in the West Indies, and then finding a way to cross the ocean. He was considerably ahead of the other students in terms of accomplishments, independent reading, and life experiences, but he was nonetheless sensible that becoming a student at such an advanced age might make him appear awkwardly slow or backwards to anyone who did not know his history.

Hamilton was born in Nevis, one of the Leeward Islands that makes up part of the British West Indies. White Europeans settled this volcanic island en masse during the early boom years of the sugar trade. Plantations, worked by slaves, made the West Indies valuable colonial possessions for the European powers. (In fact, in the mid eighteenth century, Britain's West Indian holdings were far more valuable than their American colonies.) As Hamilton explains in the Jackson letter, his maternal grandfather was a French Huguenot physician who had settled in this area around 1685, after a religious purge that expelled all Protestants from France on pain of death. In Nevis, he met and formed a relationship with an Englishwoman, though they were not legally married until their second child was expected. Hamilton's mother, Rachel Faucette, was the second youngest of their seven children.

Rachel Faucette was an intriguing woman, and many of Hamilton's finest qualities seem to have been passed down from her. Beautiful and intelligent, Faucette ought to have had her pick of suitors—European women were scarce on the island, and attractive, educated young ladies who had inherited small fortunes were even scarcer. Why her mother insisted that she marry Lavien, a Danish planter who was considerably older than her and, according to Hamilton, far less wealthy than he claimed, is difficult to understand; he must have seemed charming, though this is difficult to imagine based on the behavior he later exhibited.

Faucette's marriage to Lavien was an unhappy one practically from the start. Lavien was jealous and controlling, while Faucette was clever and strong-willed. Lavien lost all the money Faucette brought to the marriage, which must have also heightened tensions in the relationship. After five years and the birth of one child, Peter, whom

Lavien claimed was the product of Faucette having an extramarital affair, Faucette left him. Lavien was enraged by her departure, and he retaliated by having Faucette thrown into prison on charges of adultery, though there is no record of whom, precisely, she was supposed to have committed adultery with. Technically, under Danish law, Lavien was within his rights to do this, but it was considered a cruel and vindictive measure even by the standards of the time. Faucette was, in fact, the first woman in the area ever imprisoned on an adultery conviction.

The conditions in the prison where Faucette was held were barely sufficient to sustain life, being unsanitary and overheated, and the food borderline inedible. Incredibly, Lavien appears to have been under the impression that after having been the means of forcing Faucette to endure such suffering, she would be humbled and obedient after her release and return to live with him willingly like a "proper wife".

Unsurprisingly, Faucette had no inclination to do so. Once freed, she returned to her mother's home, and eventually moved with her to the nearby island of. St. Kitts, where, a few years later, she met the son of a Scottish laird, a tradesman named James Hamilton.

Alexander Hamilton's father had been raised in a castle in Scotland. As the second youngest of five sons, however, he had to make his own living, and was therefore apprenticed to a businessman as a teenager. James Hamilton was never particularly successful in this line of work, however, and his goal of making a fortune in the sugar trade and returning to Europe a wealthy man failed. After settling into life as a permanent resident of St. Kitts, James Hamilton met Rachel Faucette, and the two set up a home together. Faucette was still technically married to Lavien, as it was extremely difficult to get a divorce in the mid 18th century but the relationship that produced Alexander Hamilton and his brother

James was a marriage in all but the legal sense of the word.

It is worth mentioning here that the portion of the Jackson letter in which Hamilton claims that his parents only realized that their "marriage" was not lawful after they had begun living together is untrue, a white lie that he told to soften the irregularity of the situation. It is a characteristic demonstration of how, throughout his life, Hamilton was hypersensitive to criticism of his illegitimate birth—not at all unsurprisingly, considering how often his political enemies tried to use it against him.

Rachel Faucette and James Hamilton seem to have led a happy life together, at least for part of Hamilton's childhood. According to the account of his own grandson, "Hamilton's father does not appear to have been successful in any pursuit, but in many ways was a great deal of a dreamer, and something of a student, whose chief happiness seemed to be in the society of his beautiful and talented wife, who was in every way intellectually his superior." In 1766, when Alexander was eleven years old, James Hamilton abandoned his family. His reasons for doing so are not entirely clear. Hamilton himself attributed his father's desertion to financial embarrassment, while Hamilton biographer Ron Chernow speculates that James Hamilton may not, in fact, have been Alexander's father at all, and that he considered himself to have discharged his duty to Faucette by supporting her until her sons were old enough to help support the family.

In any event, this change in circumstances forced Faucette to take sole responsibility for the care of her two sons. She rented a two-story house, the lower floor of which she converted into a small grocery shop. Faucette had also inherited nine slaves from her mother, five women and four children, and she supplemented her income by sending them out to work and collecting their wages. This was a fairly common arrangement in the West Indies, where such a large percentage of the black population was enslaved that even comparatively poor whites could generally afford to become slave owners. Hamilton, as an adult, would be the most ardent abolitionist of all the founding fathers, and his childhood proximity to slaves and the slave trade in all its ugliness may well have played a large role in that.

Hamilton Is Orphaned

In February of 1768, at the age of 38, Rachel Faucette became bedridden with a sudden and severe fever. Her older son James was not affected, but the thirteen year old Hamilton became ill as well; he eventually recovered, but Faucette died on February 19th. Then, as if being orphaned were not sufficient hardship for two children to overcome, their mother's first husband, Johann Lavien, put in a claim to deny the boys their inheritance.

Lavien had obtained a divorce from Faucette about two years earlier, shortly before James Hamilton abandoned her. The court case had effectively destroyed her reputation, as she could no longer maintain the public pretense that she and the elder Hamilton were married. Nor could they be married afterwards, as the divorce decree forbade her from ever taking another husband.

The divorce meant that Lavien was not entitled to inherit Faucette's estate after her death; however, Faucette's oldest son, Peter Lavien, who had left the West Indies to settle in South Carolina, was entitled to at least a share. Lavien had always claimed that Peter was not his son, but after Faucette left the marriage he had raised him anyway, and after Faucette's death, Lavien brought suit on Peter's behalf. He argued that the mother's entire estate should go to her one legitimate child, rather than being shared equally with her other children—"whore-children", as Lavien termed Alexander and James.

The probate court ruled in Lavien's favor, and Peter Lavien traveled all the way back to the West Indies just to claim the fairly meager estate that Faucette left behind—a sum of money that could not have made a considerable difference to a man already respectably settled in a new life in South Carolina, but would have made a world of difference to two orphaned children. James and Alexander Hamilton lost everything they had in the world because of the ex-husband who was determined to take revenge against their mother. The only personal possessions that Alexander was allowed to keep were the thirty four books in his mother's personal library, which Faucette's cousin, James Lytton, purchased back from the estate and gave to him as a gift.

After their mother's funeral, Alexander and James were sent to live with James Lytton's son Peter; six months later, after suffering business failures, Peter Lytton committed suicide, without making any provisions for the two boys in his will. James Lytton took the Hamilton brothers in afterwards, but a mere month after his son's death, he died as well.

Fortunately for Alexander, during the short interval between his mother's death and the deaths of his cousins, he had gained employment as a clerk for Beekman and Cruger, the same trading firm that once supplied his mother with the food items she sold in her shop. His brother James was apprenticed to a carpenter, and Alexander went to live in the home of a wealthy merchant by the name of Thomas Stevens, who had five children. (The speculation as to whether James Hamilton Sr. was truly Hamilton's biological father stems from the fact that Hamilton bore an uncanny resemblance to one of Stevens's younger sons, with whom Hamilton remained close friends throughout his life.) After this separation in their circumstances, Alexander and James Hamilton's lives would take very different paths; they would see little of one another as adults.

Education and Early Accomplishments

Hamilton received little, if any, formal schooling as a boy; at least, he did not attend the Anglican schools where most of the white children on Nevis studied, possibly because he was known to be illegitimate. He received some instruction from a Jewish woman when he was a very small child, but like George Washington and several other prominent Americans of this era, Hamilton was extensively self-educated, a prodigious reader of every kind of book, who possessed a distinct flair for composition. This latter ability would turn out to be the trademark of Hamilton's career and legacy.

Hamilton would refer to the years of his trade apprenticeship at Beekman and Cruger as the most valuable period of his entire education, and it is easy to see why: it is a rare fourteen year old boy who learns how to manage an import-export business, taking inventory, keeping books, writing invoices and records, calculating prices in a number of different currencies, and setting shipping courses. He was also fluent in French from his early childhood, owing partly to his mother's French ancestry and partly to the preponderance of French-speaking businessmen selling cargo from the French West Indies. This gave him a distinct advantage during the Revolutionary War, when American officers who were capable of communicating with their French allies were in short supply.

The teenaged Hamilton was not satisfied to merely be a talented clerk, however; he knew, or believed himself, to be the grandson of a nobleman, and more to the point, he recognized that he possessed talents which would enable him to advance socially, if he was ever given the opportunity to put them to full use. His chief goal was to follow his friend Edward Stevens to New York and study at King's College (now Columbia University.) But he could afford neither the passage overseas nor the tuition. In a letter to Stevens, he wrote:

"To confess my weakness, Ned, my ambition is so prevalent that I...would willingly risk my life, tho' not my character, to exalt my station. I'm confident that my youth excludes me from any hopes of immediate preferment, nor do I desire it, but I mean to prepare the way for futurity... My folly makes me ashamed, yet Neddy we have seen such schemes successful when the projector is constant. I shall conclude saying I wish there was a war."

The wish for war may seem a peculiar one to modern readers, but in the mid eighteenth century warfare was seen differently than it is today. Clashes between countries were considered inevitable, even healthy for society in the long run, and through battlefield promotion and prizes an able young man with an officer's commission could boost his standing in society almost as far as his talents would allow. In fact, during this seafaring era in European history, hereditary nobility were wont to complain that the military had forced them to acknowledge as equals men whose grandfathers would hardly have been fit to polish their boots—the system functioned as a kind of martial meritocracy. Hamilton saw battlefield glory as his only chance to overleap the barriers of class and fortune that stood in the way of his career, and he began cherishing this ambition when he was barely more than a child.

When Hamilton was seventeen years old, a violent hurricane struck the island of St. Croix, destroying trees, buildings, homes, and ships. About a week later, Hamilton composed a letter to his father, describing the terrifying experience of living through the hurricane, and detailing the chaos and destruction left in its wake. This letter was to change Hamilton's life in ways he could not have foreseen when he wrote it. After showing the letter to his friend and religious mentor Hugh Knox, Knox asked for permission to publish it in *The Royal Danish American Gazette*, a small newspaper which had recently begun to be published on the island, and which had already published two short poems by Hamilton. Knox wrote a preface, identifying the author of the letter as a boy of seventeen.

This is considered to be a feat of astonishing literary prowess for having been written by so young a person. A sizeable excerpt appears below:

"It began about dusk, at North, and raged very violently till ten o'clock. Then ensued a sudden and unexpected interval, which lasted about an hour. Meanwhile the wind was shifting round to the South West point, from whence it returned with redoubled fury and continued so 'till near three o'clock in the morning. Good God! what horror and destruction. It's impossible for me to describe or you to form any idea of it. It seemed as if a total dissolution of nature was taking place. The roaring of the sea and wind, fiery meteors flying about it in the air, the prodigious glare of almost perpetual lightning, the crash of the falling houses, and the ear-piercing shrieks of the distressed, were sufficient to strike astonishment into Angels. A great part of the buildings throughout the Island are levelled to the ground, almost all the rest very much shattered; several persons killed and numbers utterly ruined; whole families running about the streets, unknowing where to find a place of shelter; the sick exposed to the keenness of water and air without a bed to lie upon, or a dry covering to their bodies; and our harbours entirely bare. In a word, misery, in all its most hideous shapes, spread over the whole face of the country. A strong smell of gunpowder added somewhat to the terrors of the night; and it was observed that the rain was surprizingly salt. Indeed the water is so brackish and full of sulphur that there is hardly any drinking it.

"My reflections and feelings on this frightful and melancholy occasion, are set forth in the following self-discourse.

"Where now, oh! vile worm, is all thy boasted fortitude and resolution? What is become of thine arrogance and self sufficiency? Why dost thou tremble and stand aghast? How humble, how helpless, how contemptible you now appear. And for why? The jarring of elements—the discord of clouds? Oh! impotent presumptuous fool! How durst thou offend that Omnipotence, whose nod alone were sufficient to quell the destruction that hovers over thee, or crush thee into atoms? See thy wretched helpless state, and learn to know thyself. Learn to know thy best support. Despise thyself, and adore thy God. How sweet, how unutterably sweet were now, the voice of an approving conscience; Then couldst thou say, hence ye idle alarms, why do I shrink? What have I to fear? A pleasing calm suspense! A short repose from calamity to end in eternal bliss? Let the Earth rend. Let the planets forsake their course. Let the Sun be extinguished and the Heavens burst asunder. Yet what have I to dread? My staff can never be broken—in Omnipotence I trusted.

"He who gave the winds to blow, and the lightning to rage—even him have I always loved and served. His precepts have I observed. His commandments have I obeyed—and his perfections have I adored. He will snatch me from ruin. He will exalt me to the fellowship of Angels and Seraphs, and to the fullness of never ending joys.

But alas! How different, how deplorable, how gloomy the prospect! Death comes rushing on in triumph veiled in a mantle of tenfold darkness. His unrelenting scythe, pointed, and ready for the stroke. On his right hand sits destruction, hurling the winds and belching forth flames: Calamity on his left threatening famine disease and distress of all kinds. And Oh! thou wretch, look still a little further; see the gulph of eternal misery open. There mayest thou shortly plunge— the just reward of thy vileness. Alas! whither canst thou fly? Where hide thyself? Thou canst not call upon thy God; thy life has been a continual warfare with him.

"Hark—ruin and confusion on every side. 'Tis thy turn next; but one short moment, even now, Oh Lord help. Jesus be merciful!

"Thus did I reflect, and thus at every gust of the wind, did I conclude, 'till it pleased the Almighty to allay it. Nor did my emotions proceed either from the suggestions of too much natural fear, or a conscience over-burthened with crimes of an uncommon cast. I thank God, this was not the case. The scenes of horror exhibited around us, naturally awakened such ideas in every thinking breast, and aggravated the deformity of every failing of our lives. It were a lamentable insensibility indeed, not to have had such feelings, and I think inconsistent with human nature."

On such a small island, with such a small population of educated persons, this composition could hardly avoid attracting attention and notice to its author. The letter had been published anonymously, but inquiries were made into the identity of the writer, and soon, local businessmen were making donations to a fund that would send Hamilton to America, to King's College, where his friend Edward Stevens was studying to be a doctor.

The news must have come to Hamilton as the deepest kind of relief: with the island in ruins, he would surely have found it even harder than before to pull himself up by his own bootstraps, so to speak, if he had stayed. Within a month of publishing his account of the hurricane, Alexander Hamilton was on a ship headed for New York. He would never return to the West Indies, and from that point forward in his life, he rarely mentioned any of the calamities and misfortunates that shaped his early boyhood. In America, he set out to make a new life for himself, practically a new identity, and he couldn't afford to be weighed down by the baggage of his past.

Throughout Hamilton's life, his political enemies would seize upon the scant few details that were known about his background in order to demean his character and turn public opinion against him. The fact that his parents were not married was a favorite topic of derision. His being from the West Indies made him the subject of speculation regarding his racial identity; there were an abundance of rumors about his mother, claiming, among other things, that she was a prostitute, and that she or her children were mixed race—that one of their parents or grandparents had been black. No less a person than John Adams referred to Hamilton as a "Creole bastard", suggesting that his heritage was less than perfectly white—a grave insult, portending social calamity and political ruin if it were to be believed.

There were certainly a number of illegitimate mixed race children on Nevis and St. Croix, but census records were meticulous in distinguishing between white islanders and those with even a drop of non-white blood, and it seems unlikely that Faucette or her parents could have successfully concealed such a heritage. It is, perhaps, worth mentioning, however, that Hamilton was more than merely an abolitionist:

unlike the vast majority of people in his time, abolitionists or not, Hamilton believed in racial equality, that is, that the "natural faculties" of blacks and whites were the same. By contrast, Thomas Jefferson and James Madison, owners of slaves numbering in the hundreds, were nominally interested in ending slavery—eventually—but believed that free blacks ought to be transported to the American interior, far away from white settlements, where they could never successfully merge with white society.

Chapter Two: Hamilton in America

King's College

Arriving in New York in the autumn of 1772, Hamilton was fortuitously, even providentially placed to join in with the pre-revolutionary furor that was sweeping the colonies. Only two years before, in 1770, a squad of British soldiers had fired on a crowd of civilians in the Boston Commons, an event known as the Boston Massacre. Within three more years, the Continental Congress would assemble, an army would be organized under George Washington, and open rebellion against British authority would break out. But during Hamilton's college days, the conflict was still being conducted on the level of debates and bar room brawls. This suited Hamilton's style perfectly: he was a budding orator in search of an audience, and he lost no time in making his political opinions loudly and publicly known.

Hamilton spent his first six months in America attending a preparatory academy near the College of New Jersey (now Princeton), learning Greek, Latin, and advanced math—the only subjects necessary for entry to the premier American universities that he hadn't mastered entirely on his own. He then made inquiries about studying at Princeton, proposing that he be allowed to advance through the curriculum as quickly as his abilities would allow—that is, to finish his degree in less than the normal course of three or four years. The Princeton authorities were impressed by his knowledge and intellect, but deemed Hamilton's proposal too irregular to be allowed. Hamilton chose to attend King's College (now Columbia) instead, beginning his studies some time in 1773. There, he took extra classes and tutorial sessions with the president of the college, Dr. Myles Cooper, and with a mathematics professor named Robert Harpur. Just as when he was a boy, Hamilton supplemented his education with self-directed extracurricular reading, making extravagant use of the university library.

Early Days of the Revolution

Initially, Hamilton was too focused on his rigorous, time-consuming course of study to be drawn into the political fervor that surrounded him, but he hadn't been in the country long before everyone was being forced to choose a side: patriotic or loyalist. In December of 1773, the punitive restrictions of the Stamp Act led directly to the Boston Tea Party and Paul Revere's famous midnight ride, and America began galloping headlong towards revolution. Hamilton's first, anonymous public venture into the political arena was a written defense of the destruction of British tea during the Boston harbor raid. He was on solid footing here; as a former clerk in a West Indian trade organization, he was well acquainted with the unjust effects of the Stamp Act.

The British retaliated for the Boston Tea Party by imposing a series of measures known as the Coercive, or Intolerable Acts, to be enforced until the city of Boston paid over a million dollars for the tea that had been destroyed. The Acts curtailed major civil rights that American colonists enjoyed as citizens of the British empire, and the outrage they created began, for the first time, to prompt the thirteen colonies to act as a unified political body. The first Continental Congress was assembled in the city of Philadelphia, boycotts of British goods by American merchants ensued, and in New York, anti-British societies such as the Sons of Liberty began to stage public demonstrations to rally support for the patriotic cause. It was at one such demonstration, on July 6, 1774, that Hamilton gave his first public speech in support of the American cause, advocating for the boycotts and defending Boston for its resistance to English tyranny. This put him in conflict with his King's

College mentor, Myles Cooper, who was an ardent loyalist and was deeply appalled by the revolutionary fervor that had infected his students.

Hamilton was always at his strongest and most effective as the writer of essays and polemics, and his next contribution to the revolutionary effort took the form of a thirty-five page rebuttal to a Loyalist pamphlet, which he wrote in about three weeks and published in the *New-York Gazetteer* in December of 1774. The pamphlet, written by a clergyman named Samuel Seabury, vilified the resolutions passed by the Continental Congress in the strongest possible terms; Hamilton, in turned, defended the Congress and the cause of American liberty, as only a supremely self-confident, overly bright young person could. The first three paragraphs of his rebuttal, entitled "A Full Vindication of the Measures of Congress", are excerpted below:

"It was hardly to be expected that any man could be so presumptuous, as openly to controvert the equity, wisdom, and authority of the measures, adopted by the congress: an assembly truly respectable on every account! Whether we consider the characters of the men, who composed it; the number, and dignity of their constituents, or the important ends for which they were appointed. But, however improbable such a degree of presumption might have seemed, we find there are some, in whom it exists. Attempts are daily making to diminish the influence of their decisions, and prevent the salutary effects, intended by them. The impotence of such insidious efforts is evident from the general indignation they are treated with; so that no material ill-consequences can be dreaded from them. But lest they should have a tendency to mislead, and prejudice the minds of a few; it cannot be deemed altogether useless to bestow some notice upon them.

"And first, let me ask these restless spirits, whence arises that violent antipathy they seem to entertain, not only to the natural rights of mankind; but to common sense and common modesty. That they are enemies to the natural rights of mankind is manifest, because they wish to see one part of their species enslaved by another. That they have an invincible aversion to common sense is apparent in many respects: They endeavour to persuade us, that the absolute sovereignty of parliament does not imply our absolute slavery; that it is a Christian duty to submit to be plundered of all we have, merely because some of our fellow-subjects are wicked enough to require it of us, that slavery, so far from being a great evil, is a great blessing; and even, that our contest with Britain is founded entirely upon the petty duty of 3 pence per pound on East India tea; whereas the whole world knows, it is built upon this interesting question, whether the inhabitants of Great-Britain have a right to dispose of the lives and properties of the inhabitants of America, or not?

And lastly, that these men have discarded all pretension to common modesty, is clear from hence, first, because they, in the plainest terms, call an august body of men, famed for their patriotism and abilities, fools or knaves, and of course the people whom they represented cannot be exempt from the same opprobrious appellations; and secondly, because they set themselves up as standards of wisdom and probity, by contradicting and censuring the public voice in favour of those men.

"A little consideration will convince us, that the congress instead of having "ignorantly misunderstood, carelessly neglected, or basely betrayed the interests of the colonies," have, on the contrary, devised and recommended the only effectual means to secure the freedom, and establish the future prosperity of America upon a solid basis. If we are not free and happy hereafter, it must proceed from the want of integrity and resolution, in executing what they have concerted; not from the temerity or impolicy of their determinations."

Daunting though Hamilton's rebuttal to Seabury was, it did not prevent Seabury from replying with a rebuttal of his own. Hamilton's second reply, entitled "The Farmer Refuted", was over eighty pages long and took Seabury to task as naïve and lacking any understanding of the deeper issues at stake, as the first two paragraphs demonstrate:

"I resume my pen, in reply to the curious epistle, you have been pleased to favour me with; and can assure you, that, notwithstanding, I am naturally of a grave and phlegmatic disposition, it has been the source of abundant merriment to me. The spirit that breathes throughout is so rancorous, illiberal and imperious: The argumentative part of it so puerile and fallacious: The misrepresentations of facts so palpable and flagrant: The criticisms so illiterate, trifling and absurd: The conceits so low, sterile and splenetic, that I will venture to pronounce it one of the most ludicrous performances, which has been exhibited to public view, during all the present controversy.

"You have not even imposed the laborious task of pursuing you through a labyrinth of subtilty. You have not had ability sufficient, however violent your efforts, to try the depths of sophistry; but have barely skimmed along its surface. I should, almost, deem the animadversions, I am going to make, unnecessary, were it not, that, without them, you might exult in a fancied victory, and arrogate to yourself imaginary trophies."

Hamilton published the Seabury rebuttals anonymously, as to do otherwise was to court arrest. When Myles Cooper caught wind of the rumor that he had been their author, his opinion was that no one so young could have written what he was compelled to admit were highly erudite essays, though he disagreed with the sentiments they expressed.

The Patriot

Most scholars consider the official beginning date of the American Revolutionary War to be April 18, 1775, when Massachusetts colony was declared by the British to be in a state of open rebellion, and English soldiers marched through Lexington and Concord in a raid that was intended to apprehend John Hancock and Samuel Adams. The British raid was repelled by a volunteer militia of farmers and tavern keepers know as the Minutemen, and from that moment forward the Revolution was in full sway.

Hamilton probably did not immigrate to America with any idea that in doing so he would be appropriately placed to seize the battlefield glory he had fantasized about as a young boy, but that is precisely what happened. After Lexington and Concord, militias formed rapidly throughout the colonies, and Hamilton promptly volunteered for his local company, which was comprised of most of his fellow King's College students.

Hamilton's loyalty to his new country, however, did not supersede the personal loyalty he felt towards Myles Cooper. On May 10, 1775, a group of angry revolutionary protestors gathered at King's College to remove the Cooper from his post, by violent means if necessary. Cooper was warned at the last minute and made preparations to flee the angry mob; at the same time, Hamilton got word of what was happening, and scrambled to address the mob with an improvised speech that decried the use of such violence, proclaiming that it was unworthy of the noble cause they represented. He knew that he stood no chance of changing their minds, but his goal was simply to delay them long enough for Cooper to make good his escape. It is unknown whether Cooper ever realized that he was indebted to Hamilton for this service; he fled to England on a ship the very next day.

War Begins

When the Second Continental Congress convened in May of 1775, it recognized that a state of open war was approaching, and that an American army must be raised to fight it. This was no inconsiderable task; Americans with military aspirations had always joined the British army, and because of imperial prejudice against colonial officers, few Americans were ever given the chance to rise through the ranks and gain serious command experience. The closest thing to an experienced military commander to be found in the thirteen colonies was George Washington of Virginia, who was a hero of the French and Indian War. Washington had resigned his commission in the British army years before, precisely because, as an American, he was not suffered to advance to the level that his talents deserved.

The American Continental Army ought to have been doomed from the outset. It was a volunteer force of untrained farmers, shopkeepers, tavern owners, and lowlifes. Because the Continental Congress had no power to levy taxes, it had no money to outfit or pay American troops, who supplied their own weapons and their own clothing. (The latter was almost a more serious problem than the former—by the time the first winter of the war set in, many soldiers lacked shirts and shoes, to say nothing of coats, and died of exposure and illness as a result.)

Britain's was the most powerful army in Europe at the time, and the idea that such a poorly equipped and organized group of volunteer soldiers could mount any serious offensive against them was quite ludicrous. And indeed, in the first year or so of the war, defeat seemed imminent at nearly every turn.

Alexander Hamilton probably first came to Washington's attention due to his exploits during the Battle of Manhattan, an inglorious defeat for the American army that nearly ended the war before it had begun. The arrival of a British naval ship in New York harbor provoked a panicked desertion of the city, but not before Hamilton had organized the evacuation of two dozen American cannon that would otherwise have been lost to the enemy, firing them on the British ship to cover their retreat. It was an exceptionally bold move, and it took some of the sting out of the disaster. A few months later, Hamilton was appointed as a captain of artillery, responsible for mustering his own company. He raised more than the minimum number of men and contributed to their outfitting and upkeep with his own money, an act of generosity which many wealthier officers did not take upon themselves. He was popular with his men, but a stickler for military discipline, particularly in matters of dress—something he had in common with Washington, who during the French and Indian War had purchased uniforms for his troops out of his own pocket.

On July 4, 1776, when the Continental Congress published the Declaration of Independence, thereby officially abandoning any hope of reconciling with England, Hamilton was among the New York assembly of troops to whom Washington read the document aloud. Shortly afterwards, American forces were forced to evacuate the city; despite repeated attempts, they would not retake New York until after the war's end. Though mass desertion was triggered by the British incursion, Hamilton was amongst the last of the fighters to abandon Manhattan. About six months later, after the famous Delaware river crossing and the siege of Trenton, Washington invited Hamilton to become his personal aide-de-camp: the relationship that would form out of this arrangement would have an inestimable impact on both men's lives and on the country they were helping to create.

Hamilton and Washington

Almost any young officer in Washington's army would have snapped up the opportunity to join the general's personal staff without hesitation. Proximity to the charismatic commander of the army, and duties that were generally carried out far from the line of fire, would have been considered points in favor of the job by most people. Hamilton, however, had already been offered the position of aide to other high ranking officers, such as Nathaniel Greene and Henry Knox, both of whom were highly trusted by Washington and probably responsible for recommending Hamilton for the post. Hamilton turned these offers down because there was little glory in being a secretary, compared to winning victories on the battlefield that would lead to further promotions in rank. However, when Washington's offer arrived, Hamilton was recuperating from a long illness, which may have made desk work more acceptable to him.

Hamilton was utterly invaluable to Washington as an aide: he was well-educated, highly intelligent, and did not hesitate to make decisions on his own authority that reflected the decisions Washington would have made in his place, which meant that he was able to lift a large amount of the administrative burden from the general's shoulders. They had both studied military history and theory from books, and they agreed on an instinctual level about how armies, and governments, ought to be run. On a personal level, Washington was very fond of Hamilton. They had a great deal in common—both had lost parents at an early age and been forced to take on adult responsibilities at an early age as a result. Both had been denied formal educations and made up for their deficiencies of learning with self-directed programs of reading. Washington in his youth was every bit as ambitious as Hamilton, and had attempted to gain a commission in the British navy at the same age that Hamilton was writing to his friend in New York that he wished for a war.

Washington had never been able to attend college, and his lack of higher education was a source of self-consciousness and regret. As a result, he favored young officers, like Hamilton, who placed a high value on education. And while Hamilton's irregular childhood in the West Indies would have been a strike against him in the eyes of more snobbish superior officers, Washington had an entrenched policy of promoting officers based on merit, not just breeding. His idea of a well-run army was one in which ability took precedence over family connections and background. It is doubtful that Hamilton was fully forthcoming about his troubled childhood, but Washington was uniquely suited to appreciate the strength of character and resolution that Hamilton must have possessed in order to overcome the obstacles of his early life.

Washington's preference for Hamilton was so marked that it gave rise to a rumor that Hamilton was his illegitimate son, despite the fact that Washington's one and only trip outside America was to Barbados, not Nevis, five years before Hamilton was born. Washington would have had little opportunity to father a child, as he spent almost the entire trip confined the ship with a case of smallpox, but the rumor that they were related by blood followed them for the rest of their lives.

Hamilton took such complete charge of Washington's paperwork that most of the surviving field orders Washington issued during the war are in Hamilton's handwriting. He was as much a military adviser to Washington as a secretary, and some scholars have speculated that Hamilton may have chafed somewhat in this role, imagining how he might have run the army had it all been left to his authority. Washington's other aides were generally overawed by just by being in the great general's presence—he had a great deal of reserve and natural authority, which made it difficult to separate him, as a person, from the role he played—but Hamilton was far less susceptible to Washington's charisma than most. He saw it as his duty to stay by Washington's side while he was needed, but he was itching, all the while, to return to the battlefield and take up a field command.

Laurens and Lafayette

Being on Washington's staff brought Hamilton into the orbits of two young men about his age with whom he became extremely close friends: John Laurens, son of the largest plantation owner in South Carolina, and the Marquis Gilbert de Lafayette, a French nobleman who had volunteered his services as an officer in the American army. Lafayette, like Hamilton, was one of Washington's favorite aides-de-camp. The three men had certain experiences in common that made it easy for them to see to eye. All three had lived outside of America during their childhoods—Hamilton in St. Croix and Lafayette in France, while Laurens had attended school in Geneva. Hamilton and Laurens both spoke fluent French (most American officers, including Washington, did not) which enabled them to communicate with Lafayette, whose English was halting when he first arrived. Hamilton did not have many close friendships, either before the war or after, but his attachment to Laurens, and Laurens' attachment to him, were so intense as to rival a romantic infatuation.

Above all, the three men were united by their ardent abolitionism. John Laurens's father owned more slaves than anyone else in South Carolina, but the time Laurens spent as a student in Switzerland exposed him to more liberal republican ideas. Hamilton's childhood in St. Croix was spent in painfully close proximity to the most barbaric aspects of slavery and the slave trade, while Lafayette was something of a romantic and an idealist. They agreed that, if a truly free nation was to be born form the revolution, slavery must be outlawed at the outset. The abolitionist cause would absorb the energies of all three men to the end of their lives. John Laurens was fated to die during the final days of the revolution, but before then, he asked his father to give him his inheritance in the form of an armed and equipped battalion's worth of slaves, who would be given their freedom in exchange for fighting for the revolutionary cause. Lafayette lived many decades after the war, and would eventually purchase a plantation in the Caribbean, freeing all of the slaves who worked there and re-hiring any who wished to remain for a fair wage. Hamilton's anti-slavery efforts would take the form of legislation and law reform throughout his career, as he bolstered the economy of the mercantile north in an effort to reduce American dependence on slave labor in the agrarian south.

Hamilton at Valley Forge

Hamilton was prone to repeated illnesses during the war, and was often laid up in bed for weeks at a time recovering from fevers. He was recovering from one such illness in January of 1778 when he joined Washington at his winter encampment at Valley Forge. Conditions in the camp over the winter of 1777-1778 were so inimical to life that it seems incredible that any American soldiers survived it, or were fit to continue fighting when hostilities resumed in the spring. A famous story tells of Washington catching sight of bloody footprints in the snow, left by his barefoot, frostbitten men. The story may or may not be true, but it is definitely the case that American troops were lacking in shoes and other basic clothing, as well as food, shelter, and weapons. Huge numbers of the army had deserted or died of illness, starvation, and exposure by the time Hamilton joined them in January.

Hamilton was in charge of writing to Congress in Washington's name, carrying news of the situation and demanding assistance. It was only one of a number of critical functions Hamilton performed for Washington, but he was growing increasingly impatient with his behind-the-scenes role in the war; he wanted a field command, and he resented Washington for not giving him one. It is understandable that Hamilton felt limited in his position, because even though he was an able military administrator, he was also a superb field officer. He emphasized military discipline in an effort to hold the crumbling fragments of Washington's army together. One surviving letter which Hamilton wrote to Washington in January of 1778 contains a proposed series of regulations concerning how the discipline of the camp could be improved. Of the nine regulations Hamilton proposed, three of them are quoted below:

"There are still existing in the army so many abuses absolutely contrary to the military constitution, that, without a speedy stop is put to them, it will be impossible even to establish any order or discipline among the troops.

"I would, therefore, propose the following Regulations; submitting to His Excellency the Commander-in-Chief, to distinguish such as may be published under his own authority in General Orders, and such as will require the sanction and authority of the committee of Congress now in camp.

"1stly.—Every officer or soldier who acts contrary to the Regulations for the order and discipline of the army, established by Congress, shall be tried and punished for disobedience of orders.

"2ndly.—Every officer who absents himself from his regiment without leave, shall be tried and punished. If he remains absent three weeks, he shall be ordered to join by a notification in General Orders, and in the public newspapers. And in case of his absence three weeks afterward, such notification shall be repeated. And should he not return in three weeks from the last notification, he shall, by the sentence of a court martial, be cashiered and rendered incapable of ever holding a commission in the armies of the United States.

"3rdly.—Every officer on furlough, who remains absent ten days longer than the time allowed him, shall be tried by a court martial. And in case of his being, by sickness or any other cause, detained from his regiment six days above the time allowed in his furlough, he shall inform the commanding officer of his regiment of the reasons that prevent his returning. In default of such information, he shall be notified, tried, and punished, agreeably to the second article."

It no doubt says a great deal about the state of the American army in 1778 that Hamilton felt the need to make a special regulation asserting that officers would be punished if they were to go absent without leave, something that in any professional army would be automatically understood. Fortunately, both for Hamilton's sensibilities and the fate of the revolution, in February of 1778, Washington accepted the services of a Prussian soldier who went by the name of Baron von Steuben (he was not, in fact, an actual baron), who would instill the general's army with the rigid, professional military discipline it so badly needed.

Baron von Steuben, and the Marquis de Lafayette, were by no means the only foreign military officers who came to America to offer their services to Washington. They were, however, almost the only two who did not demand exorbitant pay (which Washington could not afford), high military ranks (which Washington was unwilling to dispense), and a great deal of gratitude and deference in exchange for their help. Lafayette asked for no payment, and in fact spent a great deal of his own money on equipment and clothing for American soldiers. Steuben, likewise, asked to be paid only in the event that the Americans won the war. Once an aide to Frederick the Great of Prussia, Steuben had spent most of his adult life as a soldier in the greatest professional armies in Europe, and he had a great deal to offer the untutored Americans.

Steuben's native language was German and he spoke little English, but he was able to communicate effectively with Laurens and Hamilton in French. Together, Steuben and Hamilton would tour the camp, Steuben barking orders and Hamilton relaying them in English. With Steuben's help, Washington's army learned, for the first time, how to (in the words of historian Ron Chernow) "march in formation, load muskets, and fix bayonets [while Steuben] sprink[led] his orders with colorful *goddamns* and plentiful polyglot expletives that endeared him to the troops." Hamilton helped Steuben compile his orders in the form of a booklet, and the collection of army regulations that resulted from their collaboration would be used by the American military for the next eighty years, until after the Civil War.

The Battle of Monmouth

Hamilton had his chance to get back into the field and face the guns of the enemy when Washington ordered an attack on British forces as they retreated from the occupation of Philadelphia in June of 1778. Washington had gathered a council of officers to advise him as to the wisdom of mounting the attack, but almost all of them were opposed to it. Washington rarely overruled his officers when they were in consensus against him, but this time he did so, placing General Charles Lee in command. Lee had been one of the most vocal critics of the attack plan, and Washington would soon regret leaving it in his hands.

Due either to Lee's initial ambivalence over the attack or his general lack of competence as a commander (Hamilton attributed it to the latter), he ordered his men to retreat almost as soon as the attack order was given, the moment the British resisted with bayonets. Hamilton attempted to make up for Lee's shortcomings by dashing around the battlefield with such energy that, though his horse was shot out from under him, he still continued to fight, not pausing until he collapsed from heat stroke. When Washington found Lee retreating, he called him a "damned poltroon" (Washington scarcely ever resorted to profanities or lost his temper in public) and relieved him of his command. Mounting a white stallion, Washington led his men personally in an energetic counter-attack that kept the battle from becoming a rout.

According to Hamilton biographer Ron Chernow,

"Many people were struck by Hamilton's behavior at Monmouth, which showed more than mere courage. There was an element of ecstatic defiance, an indifference toward danger, that reflect his youthful fantasies of an illustrious death in battle. One aide said that Hamilton had shown 'singular proofs of bravery' and appeared to 'court death under our doubtful circumstances and triumphed over it'. John Adams later said that General Henry Knox told him stories of Hamilton's 'heat and effervescence' at Monmouth. At moments of supreme stress, Hamilton could screw himself up to an emotional pitch that was nearly feverish in intensity."

Washington arrested Lee for refusing his orders and subjected him to a court martial, where Hamilton made his feelings about Lee's behavior plain by giving testimony against him. In the end, Lee was found guilty and suspended from the army for a year, which effectively put a permanent end to his military career. Lee was furious and vindictive; he snubbed Hamilton outright when they met in person and whispered behind his back that Hamilton had lied in giving his testimony. Lee believed that Hamilton would eventually challenge him to a duel, but even though Hamilton was rather hotheaded, he was far more likely to defend the honor of a friend than issue a challenge on his own behalf. It was John Laurens who ultimately challenged Lee to a duel, with Hamilton serving as Laurens' second, because Lee was even more vociferous in insulting Washington than he had been in insulting Hamilton. The duel took place as scheduled, and both Lee and Laurens survived, though Lee was wounded in the right side.

Elizabeth Schuyler

At a ball which he attended in February of 1780, Hamilton renewed a slight previous acquaintance with the daughter of Revolutionary general Phillip Schuyler. Once among the most eminent senior commanders of the Continental army, Schuyler had fallen somewhat in Hamilton's estimation the previous year, when the strategically critical Ft. Ticonderoga was lost to the British; however, Schuyler had demanded a court martial to investigate his role in the matter and was cleared of wrongdoing, which seemed to elevate him in Hamilton's opinion once again. When Schuyler's wife, three sons, and four daughters came to stay in Morristown, New Jersey, near Washington's winter encampment, Hamilton began to spend a great deal of time with his family.

Hamilton was somewhat notorious for his dealings with women. He was considered handsome, not quite the same ideal of robust soldierly masculinity as Washington, but energetic and expressive, with reddish hair, a fair complexion, and eyes described as blue or violet in color. He had carried on a long flirtation with a woman named Kitty Livingston, who happened to be close friends with Elizabeth Schuyler, and may have been responsible for re-introducing them. His thoughts had turned to marriage during the course of the war, and Schuyler happened to be a close match for a description Hamilton had composed in a letter to John Laurens concerning the ideal qualities he sought in a potential wife: when he married, he said, he hoped that his bride would be young, tolerably good looking, possessed of a calm, cheerful temperament, religious but not too pious, and able to bring enough money into the marriage to make her reasonably comfortable, though it would be best if she did not care about money too much, since he doubted that he himself would ever be rich.

Elizabeth Schuyler was three years younger than Hamilton, with dark hair and large dark eyes, considered clever, sweet, and energetic by her friends. Hamilton himself described her as "unmercifully handsome and so perverse that she has none of those pretty affectations which are the prerogatives of beauty. Her good sense is destitute of that happy mixture of vanity and ostentation which would make it conspicuous to the whole tribe of fools and foplings."

In Hamilton's eyes, Schuyler's personal attractions were only enhanced by the large, happy family she belonged to: an orphan who had been alone in the world since the age of thirteen, he was thrilled to be inducted into a clan of numerous, affectionate in-laws. He became close friends with Schuyler's sisters, particularly the intelligent, talented Angelica and the brave, clever Margarita, known as Peggy. The Schuyler sisters were all forceful, dynamic personalities. Later in life, Angelica Schuyler would be connected romantically to a number of America's leading men, including Thomas Jefferson, and after the French Revolution, she helped orchestrate the Marquis de Lafayette's escape from prison. Peggy, no less resourceful, singlehandedly repelled a raid on the family home conducted by British soldiers intent on kidnapping her father; while her parents and pregnant sisters hid upstairs, she met a British soldier on the staircase and coolly informed him that she had sent for reinforcements from the villages, whereupon the soldiers fled.

A number of letters from Hamilton's courtship of Elizabeth Schuyler have been preserved, and they give testament to the profound attachment he felt after knowing her for only a few short months, as in this example, where he pleads with her to write more frequently:

"It is an age my dearest since I have received a letter from you; the post is arrived and not a line. I know not to what to impute your silence; so it is I am alarmed with an apprehension of your being ill... Sometimes my anxiety accuses you of negligence but I chide myself whenever it does. You know very well how precious your letters are to me and you know the tender, apprehensive amiable nature of my love. You know the pleasure that hearing from you gives me. You know it is the only one I am now capable of enjoying. After all you certainly would not neglect me if you possibly could. Here am I immersed in business, yet every day or two I find leisure to write to my angel; the reason is you are never out of my thoughts, and if I had but one hour in the four and twenty to rest all of it would be devoted to you. I do not say this to reproach you with unkindness. I cannot suppose you can, in so short an absence, have abated your affection; and if you even found any change, I have too good an opinion of your candour to imagine you would not instantly tell me of it.

"Pardon me my lovely girl for any thing I may have said that has the remotest semblance of complaining. If you knew my heart thoroughly you would see it so full of tenderness for you that you would not only pardon, but you would even love my weaknesses. For god's sake My Dear Betsey try to write me oftener and give me the picture of your heart in all its varieties of light and shade. Tell me whether it feels the same for me or did when we were together, or whether what seemed to be love was nothing more than a generous sympathy. The possibility of this frequently torments me."

The precise date of Hamilton's becoming engaged to Schuyler is not known, but judging from the tone of their correspondence, he seems to have proposed in late February or March of 1780, within a month of her coming to

Morristown with her family. He probably applied to her father for her hand around that time, because Schuyler wrote to Hamilton, giving his permission for the marriage, in April, indicating that he had taken a few weeks to discuss the matter with his wife.

For an orphan from the West Indies with no fortune or family background, it would have been understandable if Hamilton had been nervous about gaining the approval of Schuyler's family, as they were not only wealthy but amongst the oldest Dutch families in New York society. But Hamilton's extraordinary personal qualities, not to mention his accomplishments as a soldier and his key position on Washington's personal staff, seem to have overcome any objections they may have had—in fact, Phillip Schuyler was so fond of his daughter's suitor that he referred to him as "my beloved Hamilton".

Hamilton's relationship with Angelica Schuyler was particularly intimate. Elizabeth was not especially intellectual; she was bright and well versed in current affairs, but not bookish, and more innocent than sophisticated. Hamilton's list of attributes to be desired in a wife had not specified any particular scholarly attainments, but in his letters to Eliza he occasionally adopted a somewhat patronizing tone, urging her to read more and improve her mind. Angelica, on the other hand, was considered by those who knew her to be Hamilton's intellectual equal. They were so alike in temperament and so attached to one another that those around them commented that had she not already been married, Hamilton would probably have proposed to her instead of her sister. As it was, there was some speculation that they were having an affair. Her own husband was a staid yet wealthy businessman, considerably less clever than she. Angelica's interest in politics and current affairs had more of an outlet through Hamilton, to whom she gave valuable advice throughout his career.

The Treachery of Benedict Arnold

As Washington's right hand man, Hamilton was present for one of the most notorious events of the American Revolution: General Benedict Arnold's attempt to betray West Point to the British. Arnold had been wounded during the Battle of Ticonderoga, and as a reward had been named the military governor of Philadelphia while he recovered. During his time in the city, he entered into talks with British loyalists, probably through connections with his wife's family. After leaving Philadelphia, he was placed in command of the fort at West Point and instructed by Washington to improve its fortifications. Instead, he did precisely the opposite; in exchange for a reward of cash, a commission in the British army, and a home in England after the war, he began to sabotage the fort's defenses, making it vulnerable to attack.

In the summer of 1780, Washington, along with
Hamilton, Lafayette, and others, traveled to
West Point to examine Arnold's improvements to
the fort. Hamilton and Lafayette rode ahead of
Washington to Arnold's home; while they were
there, Arnold received a note warning him that
the British spy with whom he had been colluding
had been captured, and documents implicating
Arnold's guilt had been discovered on his person.
Unbeknownst to either of them, Hamilton had
already received a letter informing Washington
of the plot, but he had placed it amongst
Washington's other papers, and it was not
discovered until Arnold had already sneaked out
of the house and raced towards the safety of the
British lines.

Washington and his aides were in Arnold's house
with his wife and his servants when they
discovered his betrayal, which placed them in a
rather awkward position: should they question
Mrs. Arnold in the hopes of learning more about

the plot, or leave her to her own devices? In fact, Peggy Arnold knew all about her husband's defection, but she covered her involvement by pretending to have been driven mad with grief; she cried hysterically and acted as if she did not recognize Washington or his aides, asking them repeatedly if they were going to murder her and her baby.

It seems doubtful that Washington or Hamilton would have treated her harshly in any case, as they were both deeply sentimental and chivalrous where women were concerned, but as it was, they were completely taken in by her performance. Hamilton wrote to Eliza about it, saying that "her sufferings were so eloquent that I wished myself her brother to have a right to become her defender." Washington ended up giving her a letter of safe conduct and an escort that enabled her to return to her family in Philadelphia. On her way there, however, she stopped at the home of a friend, and told her the whole story of how she had pulled the wool over the eyes of Washington and all his staff. The story did not become public knowledge until years later, however, when the friend to whom Peggy Arnold had told the story married one of Hamilton's principle political rivals, Aaron Burr.

Marriage

Alexander Hamilton and Elizabeth Schuyler were married in the bride's home on December 14, 1780, less than a year after their courtship began, by a clergyman of the Dutch Reformed Church to which the Schuyler family belonged. The honeymoon lasted through the Christmas holidays. Before the wedding, Hamilton wrote several times to Phillip Schuyler, seriously discussing what was to become of the family if the British should win the war. Hamilton proposed that they should leave America and move to Geneva, where political freedom was encouraged. He also confessed that he had, at one time, "determined to let my existence and

American liberty end together"—in other words, to get himself killed in battle if it seemed that the revolution would not succeed—but that falling in love with Elizabeth had changed his mind and "given me a motive to outlive my pride." After the marriage, Hamilton wrote to his father with the news, urging him to come to America for a visit so that he could meet his new daughter-in-law. Hamilton had been corresponding with his father since shortly after James Hamilton left his family, and occasionally sent him money, but though he suggested a visit several times, the elder Hamilton never took it upon himself to make the journey.

Around the time of his marriage, Hamilton's frustrations over being confined to a secretarial position on Washington's staff came to a head. He was determined to return to the battlefield, or at least get out from behind a desk. He was nominated before Congress to become the American ambassador to France, and again to be ambassador to Russia, but he was rejected both times. The situation changed permanently in January of 1781, when Washington made a short-tempered remark to Hamilton, chiding him unfairly for keeping him waiting; Hamilton immediately walked out on him, as if he had only been waiting for an excuse to dissolve their partnership. The fact that Washington attempted to apologize and Hamilton rebuffed him demonstrates that he had reached the limit of his patience. In March of 1781 Hamilton formally resigned his position as Washington's aide. He maintained the appearance of civility with Washington in public; in private, he redoubled his applications to be appointed to a field command.

The newly married Eliza Hamilton was concerned that Hamilton would be hurt or killed if he succeeded in obtaining a command of a regiment, whereas Angelica Schuyler, who followed his career closely, was eager for him to get a promotion. Hamilton was even more eager, and finally resorted to hint to Washington that if he did not get the battlefield assignment he had been waiting for over four years, he would resign his commission. Washington had always denied him, on the grounds that he could not afford to do without Hamilton's assistance as his aide; now that Hamilton had left his staff, his only objection lay in the fact that to give Hamilton a command would mean promoting him over the heads of officers who, though possibly less capable than he, were still more entitled to command by right of seniority. The threat of Hamilton resigning his commission swayed his hand, however, and in July of 1781, Hamilton was assigned to lead a light-infantry battalion out of New York. It was perhaps the second best piece of news he received that summer, after learning the Eliza was pregnant with their first child.

The Battle of Yorktown

In September of 1781, the pivotal battle of the American Revolution was fought in Yorktown, along the James River in Virginia. Washington's decision to engage the British there was a closely held secret; the British expected that the Americans would make yet another attempt to free New York, rather than attempt to engage their army in the south. Virginia was the most densely populated American colony, holding over one-fifth of the entire American population, and the British had descended on it in full force. An American siege of Yorktown was made possible only by the assistance of the French commanders Rochambeau and de Grasse, who contributed four thousand soldiers and twenty nine ships of the line (that is, warships designed to form an unbreakable defensive line of gun power during battle) to the engagement. Washington had to march his men south towards Virginia in scattered, staggered columns in order to prevent the British in New York from getting wind of the siege and sending reinforcements south.

The English fortifications at Yorktown were organized into ten earthwork redoubts, which were essentially fortresses made by digging into the side of a hill. Two of the redoubts, numbers nine and ten, were particularly close to the American lines and thus premier targets for attack. Hamilton petitioned Washington for the opportunity to lead the attack on the redoubts, and Washington placed him in command of Laurens and Lafayette for the duration of the battle. After digging a trench the British began firing, and the combined battalions rushed the redoubt under a hail of the most torrential gunfire—observers at Yorktown said that shells and bullets darkened the sky as if the artillery were dark clouds rolling in for a thunderstorm. Hamilton's battalion captured their redoubt within ten minutes.

The capture of redoubts nine and ten allowed the American army to advance and cover the construction of a second trench, and the capture of Yorktown followed shortly after. General Lord Cornwallis surrendered to Washington on October 17, 1781. The British were remarkable bad sports about losing. Hamilton made a point of guaranteeing the safety of every soldier who surrendered, and treated the officers with honor and respect. By contrast, the British spat at the Americans as they surrendered their arms. Hamilton, on seeing this, remarked to one of his French allies, "I have seen that army so haughty in its success [that] I observed every sign of mortification with pleasure."

Family and Furlough

Once an American victory at Yorktown had been secured, the outcome of the war overall was virtually assured for the Americans—but the English stubbornly persisted in fighting for another two years, regardless. Since Hamilton's role in the Battle of Yorktown had finally won him all the renown and martial glory he had been craving, and since furthermore all the important fighting of the war was finished, he took a two month leave of absence, which he extended into an indefinite furlough. (He did not resign from the army, however, just in case the fighting heated up again.)

Hamilton returned to his home in Albany, New York, to rest and regain his health and greet the birth of his first child, born that winter. Hamilton had written to Eliza during her pregnancy, teasing her because she had not written to him as often as he had written to her; he told her that the only way she could make up for the deficiencies in her correspondence was by giving birth to a son. "You will ask me if a girl will not answer the purpose," he wrote. "By no means. I fear, with all the mother's charms, she may inherit the caprices of her father and then she will enslave, tantalize and plague one half the sex."

As it happened, Eliza Hamilton gave birth to a son on January 22, 1782, who was name Philip, in honor of his maternal grandfather. Hamilton fell deeply in love with his first son, and he wrote of him in the same teasing terms that characterized his letters about Eliza before their marriage: he declared that the boy had the qualities of a future orator, only quibbling that "if he has any fault in manners, he laughs too much."

Chapter Three: The Architect of the Young Republic

Aaron Burr

Hamilton had not quite finished his university studies before the war broke out, so his first order of business after returning home was to complete his law degree and go into practice. Rather than clerking for an older lawyer, as was typical of young men who wished to be admitted to the bar, he tutored himself out of legal textbooks. What's more, in typical over-achieving fashion, Hamilton actually compiled his own textbook of statutes and practices that focused on precedents established in New York as they differed from traditional British legal thinking. It was the first uniquely American law compendium, and despite the fact that it was the work of a student rather than an established lawyer, it was copied and passed around by the New York legal community until just a few years before Hamilton's death, when a more formal study of New York state law was made. He was finally admitted to the bar about six months after resuming his studies, in July of 1782; normally, three years of study were required, but the New York Supreme Court made exceptions for students whose education had been interrupted by military service. This allowance was granted as a result of a petition made by another young officer about Hamilton's age: Aaron Burr.

Burr was the maternal grandson of America's most famous evangelical minister, Jonathan Edwards, who wrote such famous sermons as "Sinners in the Hands of an Angry God". Edwards propagated principles of Calvinist theology that would shape religious culture and practice in New England for decades to come. His son was Aaron Burr, Sr., who was president of the College of New Jersey, where Burr applied for admittance as a student at the age of 11. (He was denied, but re-applied at the age of 13, asking to be admitted as a junior; by way of compromise, he was allowed to enter as a sophomore.) Burr, like Hamilton, was studying law before the revolution, and had left his studies to join the army.

During the war, Burr, again like Hamilton, served for a brief time on Washington's personal staff, though he left this position after a brief time. He seemed to dislike Washington and was prone to speak disparagingly of his abilities, which would have negative repercussions for Burr's later political career. He even served as General Henry Lee's second when he was challenged to a duel with John Laurens for insulting Washington after the Battle of Monmouth; Hamilton, as we have discussed, was Laurens' second.

Like Hamilton (and many other soldiers) Burr suffered severe heat stroke at Monmouth; unlike Hamilton, Burr was rendered unfit for further battlefield action by his illness, though he engaged in espionage on Washington's behalf during his recovery. Burr was also married in 1782, to Theodosia Prevost, widow of a British officer, who happened to be the friend to whom Benedict Arnold's wife Peggy related the story of how she had deceived Washington and all his staff into believing her innocent of any involvement in Arnold's attempt to sell West Point to the British. They had a daughter, named Theodosia, born the year after Philip Hamilton's birth.

Burr was admitted to the bar in New York in 1782, the same year as Hamilton, and though it seems likely that they must have met before the war, this was the period during which their social circles began to overlap in a manner that must have thrust them continually into each other's path. Their careers would parallel one another for the twenty years or so, until the presidential

election of 1800 brought them into direct
contention.

Hamilton the Politician

In 1782, shortly before the war came to its
drawn-out end, John Laurens was killed in South
Carolina when he led his battalion into an attack
on a group of British soldier who were foraging
for supplies. His death was a source of immense
personal grief for Hamilton, who deeply
lamented that his friend never had the chance of
creating the first all-black free battalion, which
had been the cause nearest to his heart. Lauren's
passing marked a change in the tone of
Hamilton's life: once romantic and youthfully
idealistic, he metamorphosed into a hardened
political entity, a role he would serve for the rest
of his life. He would always be somewhat aloof
from those outside his family, and he never had
another friend with whom he enjoyed the same
kind of intimacy that he did with John Laurens.

It was as a New York delegate to Congress that Hamilton first took a public stance as a proponent of strong central government with strong ideological ties to the political, economic, and legal systems of Britain. There was a fashion, in the early days of the republic, to dispense with anything that smacked remotely of Englishness, and to come up with entirely new American systems. Hamilton, however, believed that the time-honored organizational systems used by the British government since the Tudor era were too functional and useful to be thrown out, when Americans had yet to come up with anything superior. He was by no means a British loyalist, but he would be accused throughout his lifetime and beyond of conspiring to sell the new nation to the British, or install a monarchy in place of a republican government.

Most people in the early republic were not nationalists, but regionalists, in the sense that their first loyalty was to their state, not to the country as a whole. This philosophy was reflected by the Articles of Confederation, the document that preceded the Constitution, which, during the war, had served to facilitate just enough cooperation between the colonies to allow for the creation of an army. But as Washington's former aide, Hamilton had firsthand experience with the failures of the confederation system: more than anyone except Washington himself, he knew how much the army had been shortchanged because Congress did not have the authority to collect taxes. Individual states were on their honor to pay the amount they had pledged to the support of the army, but because Congress could not force them to do as they had promised, the payments were rarely made. As far as Hamilton was concerned, a large percentage of American soldiers had frozen or starved to death because Congress could not collect taxes. He believed that even more disasters were facing the new nation unless the loose assembly of sovereign states was replaced by a unified government with central authority that could counteract state authority.

To many Americans, particularly in the south, a strong central government was just another form of monarchism, which fueled the rumors that Hamilton was a covert British agent. But others—particularly Washington, and for a time, James Madison, supported Hamilton's position. Federalist thinkers dominated American politics during the writing of the Constitution and most of Washington's two terms as president, when the new government was first taking shape.

Amongst the founding fathers, Hamilton was the foremost financial thinker. Before the revolution, all banking in America had been through England; the first American bank was not established until the Bank of North America opened in Philadelphia in 1781. During the war, Hamilton had thought deeply on the problem of currency and inflation. Each state was issuing its own bills, the rate of exchange differed across the country, and gold and silver, or else English pounds, were still considered the only hard, stable currency. The Bank of New York, which Hamilton helped to organize in June of 1784, helped regulate the new American dollar, and set the precedent for the national bank he would build as the new nation's first treasury secretary.

In April 1786, Hamilton was elected to the New York General Assembly, partly due to his political rivalry with New York governor George Clinton, long-time enemy of Hamilton's father-in-law, Philip Schuyler. As the executive in charge of one of the most powerful and wealthy states in the union, Clinton was ardently opposed to sacrificing any state autonomy to the authority of a central government. The fame Hamilton achieved by opposing Clinton openly led directly to his being named one of the New York delegates to the Continental Congress in

May of the following year, where the Articles of Confederation would be amended and reformed.

The New York delegation was split along political lines, with Hamilton as the junior member and the only Federalist. He was one of the youngest men in attendance, and for the first few weeks of the convention he exhibited uncharacteristic restraint, sitting quietly and listening to the other delegates make speeches. When Hamilton at last broke his silence, however, it was in epic fashion.

James Madison and Edmund Randolph of Virginia had proposed a plan for the structure of the new government that involved a legislative body with two houses, term limits for elected officials, and a recall mechanism to remove officials who were not performing their duties ably. Critically for the future of the country, the Virginia Plan also introduced the concept of proportional representation in the lower house. Madison and Randolph were answered by Governor William Paterson of New Jersey, who introduced a competing plan for the government, in which both legislative houses were proportionally represented; when this plan proved unpopular, he suggested a single legislative house in which each state was represented by a single person with a single vote.

Hamilton seems to have kept silent during the debate because he was taking careful notes on both plans and formulating his own alternative. By June 18, 1787, he had finished gathering his thoughts, and he proceeded to present them to Congress over the course of a six-hour speech. In Hamilton's plan, there were two legislative houses, with the lower house having elected representatives who served three year terms, and the upper house having elected representatives who served life-time terms. Most shockingly, in Hamilton's vision of government, the executive—

called, not the president, but the governor—
should be elected for life and possess absolute
veto power over legislation, while the national
legislature should choose the state governors,
whose authority was utterly subject to that of the
federal government.

Called the "British plan" by some for the close
resemblance it bore to the structure of English
government, Hamilton's plan never had a serious
chance of being adopted by Congress. The few
delegates who actually sat through all six hours
of the speech judged it bold and brilliant, but not
practical in American society. Some were
actually swayed to Hamilton's argument for a
president who served for life "upon good
behavior". After all, hereditary transmission of
power carried risks, but placing the government
in the hands of one person who would carry out
his duties until death had, throughout history,
always been the best means of ensuring national
stability. However, this was far too much like

having a king for most people's tastes. The rumors that Hamilton was a closet monarchist who was secretly trying to sell the United States back to England probably had their origins in his speech to the Constitutional Convention.

Tied to the issue of state versus federal authority was the hotly divisive topic of slavery. The revolution had triggered a wave of anti-slavery and abolitionist sentiment, and by the mid 1780's every state in New England had devised a plan for the immediate or gradual ending of slavery within its borders. New York, New Jersey, and the south, however, were still major centers for the slave trade, and the economy of the southern states was absolutely dependent on slave labor to keep its tobacco and cotton plantations in operation.

The northern delegates, practically to a man, hoped to write a ban on slavery into the

Constitution, and even southerners like Jefferson, Madison, and Washington supported language that banned the slave trade. But the south held so much of the nation's population and wealth that northern delegates feared that the Constitution would never be ratified if they did not bow to their wishes on the matter of slavery. In the end, the Constitution banned the importation of slaves after 1808, sixteen years in the future; it also determined that each slave would count for 3/5ths of a white person in the state census, which lowered tax rates for the southern states (where the slave population often equaled or outstripped the white population), but also cut down on their representative voting power. Hamilton himself conceded that such compromises were essential to the formation of the union.

Hamilton never succeeded in gaining the cooperation of the other two New York delegates, and as a consequence, New York was the last state in the union to ratify the Constitution; in fact, it was widely joked that the Constitution had been ratified by "twelve states and Colonel Hamilton."

The Federalist Papers

Throughout Hamilton's political career, he was the focus of vitriolic personal attacks from his opponents, who usually published them anonymously in newspapers. All the major political players of the day traded barbed remarks and satirical sketches in essay and pamphlet form, but Hamilton's tendency to speak his mind loudly and often provoked an unusual degree of viciousness even by the standards of the day. It didn't help that he was easy pickings, to some degree, because of his background. Essays published by partisans of George Clinton depicted a Hamilton-like character who was mixed race, from the West Indies, and the secret bastard son of George Washington. Hamilton rarely answered attacks on the circumstances of his birth, but they affected him deeply.

Hamilton was the most prolific writer of the revolutionary generation. In 1787, while others were penning thinly veiled comic caricatures of his person, he was hard at work on a series of essays that would define the relationship between the American people and the Constitution. The purpose of the Federalist Papers was to persuade the state of New York to ratify the Constitution, but Hamilton did not hesitate to enlist contributions from elsewhere in the country. He invited John Jay, James Madison, William Duer, and Governeur Morris to join the project, but only Jay and Madison took him up on it. Jay was too ill with rheumatism to pen more than five of the essays, so the bulk of the work was done by Madison and Hamilton, who published jointly under the pseudonym "Publius". Madison wrote twenty-nine of the papers, while Hamilton wrote fifty-one in the course of seven months. The results were far more ambitious and far-reaching than the original modest plan of writing twenty or twenty-five essays.

In the following extract from the first of the essays, Federalist No. 1, Hamilton explains the topics that will be covered in the course of the series, and his intentions in writing about them:

"Yes, my countrymen, I own to you that, after having given it an attentive consideration, I am clearly of opinion it is your interest to adopt it. I am convinced that this is the safest course for your liberty, your dignity, and your happiness. I affect not reserves which I do not feel. I will not amuse you with an appearance of deliberation when I have decided. I frankly acknowledge to you my convictions, and I will freely lay before you the reasons on which they are founded. The consciousness of good intentions disdains ambiguity. I shall not, however, multiply professions on this head. My motives must remain in the depository of my own breast. My arguments will be open to all, and may be judged of by all. They shall at least be offered in a spirit which will not disgrace the cause of truth.

"I propose, in a series of papers, to discuss the following interesting particulars: -- The utility of the UNION to your political prosperity -- The insufficiency of the present Confederation to preserve that Union -- The necessity of a government at least equally energetic with the one proposed, to the attainment of this object -- The conformity of the proposed Constitution to the true principles of republican government -- Its analogy to your own state constitution -- and lastly, The additional security which its adoption will afford to the preservation of that species of government, to liberty, and to property.

"In the progress of this discussion I shall endeavor to give a satisfactory answer to all the objections which shall have made their appearance, that may seem to have any claim to your attention.

"It may perhaps be thought superfluous to offer arguments to prove the utility of the UNION, a point, no doubt, deeply engraved on the hearts of the great body of the people in every State, and one, which it may be imagined, has no adversaries. But the fact is, that we already hear it whispered in the private circles of those who oppose the new Constitution, that the thirteen States are of too great extent for any general system, and that we must of necessity resort to separate confederacies of distinct portions of the whole. This doctrine will, in all probability, be gradually propagated, till it has votaries enough to countenance an open avowal of it. For nothing can be more evident, to those who are able to take an enlarged view of the subject, than the alternative of an adoption of the new Constitution or a dismemberment of the Union. It will therefore be of use to begin by examining the advantages of that Union, the certain evils, and the probable dangers, to which every State will be exposed from its dissolution."

The purpose of the Federalist Papers was to persuade the New York legislature to ratify the Constitution and thereby become an official part of the United States. The problem was that New York was one of the most powerful former colonies in America, and Governor George Clinton and his faction were adamantly opposed to the formation of a central government that would limit his autonomy. Hamilton hoped that an energetic, thorough, and reasoned defense of the Constitution would help to counteract Clinton's influence. New Yorkers in general were pro-union; in fact, there was such a pronounced split between the city of New York and the rest of the state that Hamilton conjectured that if Clinton did not change his stance, New York might secede and join the union as an independent free city. This outraged Clinton and made him an even more entrenched opponent, but gradually Hamilton's arguments began to sway members of Clinton's cabal to the federalist camp. At last, on July 26, 1788, New York joined the Union, the last of the three outlier states to do so, after North Carolina and Rhode Island.

The Election of 1788

With the union fully formed and the Constitution ratified, the next order of business for the new government was to elect a president. As far as Hamilton was concerned, George Washington was the only possible man for the job. He was not alone in this opinion: the executive powers section of the Constitution had been written with Washington in mind, and many of those who had resisted ratifying the Constitution had ultimately done so only because it was assumed Washington would be in charge of the new government.

As far as his contemporaries were concerned, Washington was the only man who could be trusted to wield the powers of the presidency without overstepping the democratic limits that distinguished him from a European king. He had proved that he was capable of such restraint when, after the war, he had resigned as head of the army rather than pressing his military advantage to make himself the head of the civilian government. Congress, under the Articles of Confederation, functioned as a committee more than a governing body, and its leaders had no authority to speak for the whole country. It had therefore fallen to Washington, as commander of chief, to function as the de facto head of the American state before such a state really existed. Observers in England and France took it for granted that Washington would transition seamlessly into a presidential or monarchial role after the war's end; European history, after all, was full of military conquerors who assumed supreme power after deposing a previous system of government. When, instead,

Washington quietly stepped down and returned to private life at his plantation, Mount Vernon, the entire world was thunderstruck by his modesty and virtue. Only such a man, with his proven record of subordinating personal gain and ambition for the good of his country, could be trusted to lead the fragile new democracy.

Hamilton knew Washington too well after serving as his aide for so many years to feel the same degree of awe and reverence for him that many others did. But even though their parting during the war had not been completely amicable, their trust in one another was still absolute. Furthermore, Hamilton knew that his own political career had been built, in large part, on his association with Washington; if Washington became president, Hamilton could rely on his old patron to place him in an influential position in his administration. The fact that Hamilton was manifestly capable of helping to shape the new government would make an appointment by Washington something more than nepotism, but there was no guarantee he would be included at the highest levels of decision-making without him. Hamilton was already making bitter political enemies after his efforts to get the Constitution ratified in New York, and he needed Washington's support if he was to wield influence.

Knowing that Washington was more ambitious than most people realized, but that he was also extraordinarily cautious of being *perceived* as ambitious, Hamilton took it upon himself to persuade Washington that he had an inescapable duty to run for the presidency. Washington understood why his services were needed, but in order to maintain the appearance of modesty, and thus preserve the trust that others had in him, he needed to let someone else talk him into running. Hamilton, no less sensitive than Washington to the delicacy of his position, sent him copies of the Federalist Papers, and wrote to him of the dangers that would result if he did not run. George Clinton of New York was also interested in the office, and his election would be a disaster for the country. He would never win against Washington, however, so it was absolutely necessary for Washington to declare his willingness to serve.

Hamilton made one disastrous misstep during the 1788 election that would have severe repercussions for his later career: he alienated John Adams, who was running for vice-president. Adams and Hamilton did not know each other well, as Adams was of an older generation, and had served in Congress and conducted negotiations in France while Hamilton was fighting in the war. After the revolution was won, Adams was dispatched to serve as the first ambassador of the United States to Great Britain. Hamilton and Adams were each aware of the other's reputation, and for Hamilton's part, he regarded Adams as an intelligent and capable public servant who would serve ably as the nation's first vice-president.

However, the election process as laid out in the Constitution posed a delicate potential problem: the person with the most votes was entitled to be president, and the person who came in second was automatically the vice-president. This meant that if the candidate for vice-president received the most votes, he would be president, regardless of whether he had been aiming for that office. Hamilton was afraid that George Clinton would manage to split the vote for Washington, and that the majority of votes would go to Adams, who, he felt, could not possibly unite the new nation under his leadership.

Hamilton's solution was to privately approach several members of the Senate and ask them not to vote for Adams. His precautions turned out to be unnecessary, as Adams received nowhere near enough votes for the presidency, even discounting the votes Hamilton had turned against him. But Adams was mortified that he hadn't received more votes; he felt that to be elected vice-president by so slim a margin was nearly worse than not being elected at all. When he learned that Hamilton had actively campaigned against him, he was furious. Hamilton, in turn, felt that Adams had misinterpreted his motivations, but it was too late to mend the breach. Adams, though a Federalist like Hamilton, would carry a grudge against him for the rest of his life. This would prove disastrous in later years, when Federalist disunity resulted in the near destruction of the party.

Chapter Four: Washington's Cabinet

Treasury Secretary

Even with a Constitution and a president firmly established, the United States occupied an awkward position in the eyes of the world during its first years of existence. Whether the nation would endure, or else crumble into anarchy and be re-conquered by England or overtaken by another European power, remained to be seen. Matters of foreign policy and finance had yet to be attended to. Washington was singlehandedly in charge of American affairs for the best part of a year after his election. There was as yet no precedent for the establishment of an executive cabinet, and the government had yet to be organized into departments with special oversight of particular areas of policy.

In the midst of Washington's first term of office, he organized three governmental departments with special oversight of particular areas of policy: a department of state, a department of war, and a department of treasury. Thomas Jefferson, still serving as the American minister in France, was asked to head the State Department, and Henry Knox, one of Washington's most trusted colleagues during the revolution, was asked to head the Department of War. Washington initially asked Robert Morris, who had handled the army's finances during the war, to be Secretary of the Treasury. Morris, however, declined the honor, and when Washington asked him to recommend another person, Morris told him that no man but Hamilton could do the job. Washington was surprised; he knew Hamilton to be intelligent and capable, but somehow, he had never heard that Hamilton was an expert in matters of finance. Morris assured him that Hamilton was exceptionally qualified, and Washington offered him the post shortly after he was elected.

Hamilton believed that the United States could not exist on equal footing with other nations of the world until it began to repay its debts, which it was not doing; the government was so penniless that it had ceased even to pay the interest on its pre-war and wartime debts. In order to cease being penniless, the government would need to collect taxes, a unique challenge for the first American Treasury Secretary; taxation was a sensitive topic in a country which had recently gone to war over unfair taxes levied by the British. For southerners and others proto-Republicans, the notion of paying any kind of tax to a central government rankled deeply.

Hamilton was warned that he would be deeply unpopular if he accepted the Treasury position, but he replied simply that "it is the situation in which I can do most good." In the words of Ron Chernow, "everything Hamilton planned to transform America into a powerful, modern nation-state—a central bank, a funded debt, a mint, a customs service, manufacturing subsidies, and so on—was to strike critics as a slavish imitation of the British model." Like most positions in the new government, the post of Treasury Secretary paid very little, but Hamilton's rigorous personal honesty was such that he turned his law practice over to a friend and devoted himself solely to the job at hand, though no one else in the cabinet dreamed of trying to get by solely on their paltry government salaries. Hamilton was thirty four years old when he took up his post on September 11, 1789.

As soon as Hamilton was named Treasury Secretary, Congress asked him for a report on public credit in America. Hamilton responded by amassing a wealth of minutely detailed information about revenue in the thirteen states and writing a document that stands today as one of his most enduring accomplishments. Hamilton's *Report on Public Credit* does more than summarize the state of the nation's finances; it lays out a guiding vision for the American financial system that is, in essence, still functional today. Most crucially for the post-revolutionary era, Hamilton proposed that the debts of the thirteen states should be assumed by the federal government, and the debt funded by the Treasury, with interest and principal paid in intervals. On January 14, 1790, Hamilton presented his report to Congress, and in the following excerpt, he establishes the principles of American debt management:

"In the opinion of the Secretary, the wisdom of the House, in giving their explicit sanction to the proposition which has been stated, cannot but be applauded by all, who will seriously consider, and trace through their obvious consequences, these plain and undeniable truths.

"That exigencies are to be expected to occur, in the affairs of nations, in which there will be a necessity for borrowing.

"That loans in times of public danger, especially from foreign war, are found an indispensable resource, even to the wealthiest of them.

"And that in a country, which, like this, is possessed of little active wealth, or in other words, little monied capital, the necessity for that resource, must, in such emergencies, be proportionably urgent.

"And as on the one hand, the necessity for borrowing in particular emergencies cannot be doubted, so on the other, it is equally evident, that to be able to borrow upon good terms, it is essential that the credit of a nation should be well established.

"For when the credit of a country is in any degree questionable, it never fails to give an extravagant premium, in one shape or another, upon all the loans it has occasion to make. Nor does the evil end here; the same disadvantage must be sustained upon whatever is to be bought on terms of future payment.

"From this constant necessity of borrowing and buying dear, it is easy to conceive how immensely the expenses of a nation, in a course of time, will be augmented by an unsound state of the public credit.

"To attempt to enumerate the complicated variety of mischiefs in the whole system of the social economy, which proceed from a neglect of the maxims that uphold public credit, and justify the solicitude manifested by the House on this point, would be an improper intrusion on their time and patience.

"In so strong a light nevertheless do they appear to the Secretary, that on their due observance at the present critical juncture, materially depends, in his judgment, the individual and aggregate prosperity of the citizens of the United States; their relief from the embarrassments they now experience; their character as a People; the cause of good government.

"If the maintenance of public credit, then, be truly so important, the next enquiry which suggests itself is, by what means it is to be effected? The ready answer to which question is, by good faith, by a punctual performance of contracts. States, like individuals, who observe their engagements, are respected and trusted: while the reverse is the fate of those, who pursue an opposite conduct.

Hamilton was not arguing that the nation should exist in a state of permanent indebtedness, though he was—and is still—interpreted that way by his critics. Debt became the issue over which Hamilton's collaborator on the Federalist Papers, James Madison, finally turned again him. Madison attacked Hamilton's credit report before Congress, saying, "I go on the principle public debt is a public curse".

Hamilton was deeply distressed by Madison's defection. They had written the Federalist Papers together based on the principle that too much unregulated power in the hands of the states was a threat to the nation, but Madison seemed now to believe that the federal government was a threat to state autonomy. The loss of Madison as an ally was more than just personally distressing for Hamilton; it was also the beginning of the end of the idealistic post-revolutionary era in American politics. From being united against England and behind George Washington, Congress was now dividing along fault lines: north vs. south, state autonomy vs. federal authority, and eventually, Hamiltonian Federalists vs. Jeffersonian Republicans.

The Return of Thomas Jefferson

After serving five years as the American ambassador to France, Thomas Jefferson returned to the United States in March of 1790 to serve as George Washington's Secretary of State. Jefferson and Hamilton had no previous acquaintance with each other; Jefferson belonged to the same generation of statesmen as John Adams, and had been working on the Declaration of Independence when Hamilton was a soldier not yet on Washington's staff. Jefferson was in France while Hamilton was making a name for himself as a hero of the revolution and a dominant presence in New York politics, though he had heard of Hamilton from another source.

In Europe, Jefferson had become acquainted with Angelica Church, Elizabeth Hamilton's sister. Church's husband was a member of Parliament and the couple's social circle included the highest-ranking members of British society, such as the Prince Regent, soon to be King George IV. One of Church's closest friends, Maria Cosway, was having an affair with the widowed Jefferson, and Church sometimes passed messages between them. Jefferson attempted to interest Church in having an affair with him herself, but she seems not to have been interested in furthering the relationship, particularly after Jefferson returned to America, where he almost immediately began to lock horns with Hamilton. Angelica Church was inveterately loyal to her brother in law, and the stories she passed on to Hamilton about Jefferson's conduct in Europe—where he espoused high-minded egalitarian ideals but lived the life of a self-indulgent aristocrat—probably influenced Hamilton's reaction to Jefferson politically.

As a Virginian and a wealthy plantation owner, Jefferson was like Madison, a privileged southerner who bemoaned the evil of slavery without taking any measures to make the southern economy less dependent upon it. And he was thoroughly approving of the French

Revolution, which was breaking out in Paris around the same time he was re-entering the world of American politics. He saw the French Revolution as a natural offshoot of the revolution in America, and considered the terrifying bloodshed a fair price for the dismantling of the monarchist regime.

Jefferson admired France and loathed England, and he was among those who perceived Hamilton as importing all the old corruptions of the British system to sully the pristine new American government. He supported Washington, but he disliked strong central government and felt that the executive powers reserved to the president were too far-reaching. This made him natural allies with James Madison, with whom he joined forces to oppose Hamilton's plan to have the federal government assume the debts of the individual states.

The American Capital

Hamilton failed in his first attempt to gain Congressional approval for his assumption-of-debt plan. Compromise of some kind was clearly necessary, but he was incapable of compromising the principles of the plan itself. He decided instead to give ground on a different issue, in order to secure the necessary votes from southern legislators.

At the time, the site of the nation's official capital city had yet to be settled. During the Constitutional Convention, the delegates had agreed to set aside a ten by ten mile area for the executive mansion and the Senate and Congressional buildings, but where those ten square miles were to be located, the Convention left to be decided later. During the war, Philadelphia had been the nation's de facto capital, as it had played host to the Continental Congress. As one of the largest and wealthiest cities in America, it was a popular choice for the permanent capital. However, Washington was presently running the government from a rented mansion in New York, making it another popular and logical option, while southerners in Congress were advocating for a site along the Potomac River in Virginia, close to Washington's home, Mount Vernon.

No one could agree whether the capital ought to be located in the equidistant center of the country, or in the nation's most populous region, or whether other factors should be taken into account. The proposal to set a ten square mile area aside as the seat of government offended the anti-monarchist paranoia of some Congressmen, who feared that the city would become the equivalent or Versailles or Westminster, a kind of royal court. In the eighteenth century, before railroads and cars and planes made travel to distant cities a matter of ease, there was considerable fear that, wherever the capital was located, the state that hosted it would become disproportionately powerful.

Hamilton was naturally an advocate for the capital being located in New York, already the nation's financial center and arguably its cultural center. But to his mind, it was far more important to the nation's future to secure the necessary number of votes in Congress to pass his debt plan.

How precisely Hamilton secured his compromise is a matter of some conjecture. According to Jefferson, he encountered Hamilton one night pacing despondently in front of Washington's front door. When Jefferson inquired what was troubling him, Hamilton placed himself at his mercy, saying that Jefferson's support was critical to gaining the Congressional approval he needed. A few days later, Jefferson invited Hamilton to a private dinner at his home along with James Madison and a few others. The result of the unspecified negotiations that took place during that dinner was that the Residence Act was passed by Congress on July 10, 1790, naming Philadelphia as the temporary site of the nation's capital while construction began of a permanent capital on the Potomac site. In return, southern votes became available for the passage of Hamilton's debt plan.

Hamilton's colleagues in New York were not impressed that he had bargained away the city's right to be the nation's capital. Curiously, in later years, Jefferson also confessed himself deeply displeased by the results of their bargain. In retrospect, Hamilton's debt plan placed so much power in the hands of the federal government that even having the nation's capital located in the south seemed to him like a poor trade off. Hamilton, however, was elated. He wrote that, "Whoever considers the nature of our government with discernment will see that though obstacles and delays will frequently stand in the way of the adoption of good measures, yet when once adopted, they are likely to be stable and permanent. It will be far more difficult to undo than to do." By passing the assumption plan, Hamilton had set the course for the future; even when Jefferson became president a decade later, he was helpless to reverse the advances that Hamilton had made with his assistance.

A National Bank

One of the most important results of Hamilton's deal to pass assumption in exchange for moving the capital south was the creation of the Bank of the United States. As an immigrant to America who lacked established roots in any particular state, Hamilton inhabited a unique perspective that elevated him above regionalism and prompted him to consider the good of the union as a whole. But even so, he had adopted New

York as his home, and as a New Yorker, he felt that the nation's future lay in business, commerce, and urban development. This widened the ideological rift between himself and Jefferson and Madison, who, as southerners, felt that the United States should develop along agricultural lines. Despite the fact that the south's cotton and tobacco based economy made it dependent upon slave labor, Jefferson believed that expanding its agricultural society was the only way to secure freedom for its people. Neither Jefferson, Madison, nor John Adams had a strong understanding of finance, and they considered Hamilton's insistence on developing the national economy suspicious, liable to import European corruption into their republican utopia. Hamilton, by contrast, felt that the best safeguard of American freedom was to make it financially viable in the world market.

Hamilton's bill to charter the national bank passed Congress in January of 1791, but the vote exposed the ideological split between north and south; virtually all northerners voted for the bank and all the southerners voted against it. Opponents of the bank believed that it would place too much power in the hands of northern merchants, and southern farmers would be at their mercy. James Madison was so convinced that the bank would be the ruin of the south that he asked Washington to use his executive power of veto for the first time in the government's history, on the ground that the bank was a violation of Constitutional law. Washington responded by gathering a committee to study the Constitution in minute detail and form an opinion as to whether the bank was indeed legal.

Hamilton's contention was that the language of the Constitution provided a liberal basis for justifying any measure that Congress saw fit to undertake for the good of the nation. He referred to Article I, section 8, clause 18, which is sometimes known as the "Necessary and Proper

Clause", or the "Elastic Clause", as the foundation for his argument. The text of that clause is below:

"The Congress shall have Power ... To make all Laws which shall be necessary and proper for carrying into Execution the foregoing Powers, and all other Powers vested by this Constitution in the Government of the United States, or in any Department or Officer thereof."

Essentially, Hamilton felt that Congress had the authority to introduce and vote on any measure not explicitly prohibited elsewhere in the Constitution, so long as it was for the country's benefit. Jefferson, unsurprisingly, took a far more conservative view: he felt that the clause ought to be interpreted far more strictly, to prevent the federal government from over-reaching.

Washington gathered the objections of his advisers and presented them to Hamilton for commentary; Hamilton's response was, in typical fashion, a fifteen-thousand word treatise on the subject of implied versus express powers in the Constitution. Jefferson had argued that the words "necessary and proper" should be interpreted to mean something more like "essential and unavoidable"; Hamilton responded that it was impossible to have a strict, objective test for what was "essential", because interpretations would always vary. To him, it made more sense to read "necessary" as "appropriate"—meaning, in other words, that Congress had license to do whatever it judged beneficial. He elaborates on this point in the following excerpt from his "Opinion as to the Constitutionality of the Bank of the United States":

"It is not denied that there are implied well as express powers, and that the former arc as effectually delegated as the latter. And for the sake of accuracy it shall be mentioned, that there is another class of powers, which may be properly denominated resting powers. It will not be doubted, that if the United States should make a conquest of any of the territories of its neighbors, they would possess sovereign jurisdiction over the conquered territory. This would be rather a result, from the whole mass of the powers of the government, and from the nature of political society, than a consequence of either of the powers specially enumerated.

"But be this as it may, it furnishes a striking illustration of the general doctrine contended for; it shows an extensive case in which a power of erecting corporations is either implied in or would result from, some or all of the powers vested in the national government. The jurisdiction acquired over such conquered country would certainly be competent to any species of legislation.

"To return: It is conceded that implied powers are to be considered as delegated equally with express ones. Then it follows, that as a power of erecting a corporation may as well be implied as any other thing, it may as well be employed as an instrument or mean of carrying into execution any of the specified powers, as any other instrument or mean whatever. The only question must be in this, as in every other case, whether the mean to be employed or in this instance, the corporation to be erected, has a natural relation to any of the acknowledged objects or lawful ends of the government. Thus a corporation may not be erected by Congress for superintending the police of the city of Philadelphia, because they are not authorized to regulate the police of that city. But one may be erected in relation to the collection of taxes, or to the trade with foreign countries, or to the trade between the States, or with the Indian tribes; because it is the province of the federal government to regulate those objects, and because it is incident to a general sovereign or legislative power to regulate a thing, to employ all the means which relate to its regulation to the best and greatest advantage."

It is arguable that Hamilton's carefully researched and reasoned commentary on implied versus express powers in the Constitution was as critical to the future of the United States as the establishment of the Bank itself. Scholars of Constitutional law continue to rely on Hamilton's interpretation of the "necessary and proper" clause to this day.

Maria Reynolds

Of all Hamilton's many political innovations, the one he was perhaps least proud of was starring in the new nation's first public sex scandal involving a government figure. Such escapades amongst politicians are commonplace now, but a greater appearance of respectability was demanded of public figures in the late eighteenth century, and its effect on Hamilton's career was disastrous.

In the summer of 1791, Hamilton's career was at its zenith, and his propensity to overwork was at its most exaggerated. His family, including Elizabeth Hamilton, their four children, and a young orphaned girl they were fostering, had moved to the temporary national capital of Philadelphia to be near him while he worked. But in the eighteenth century, warm weather in large cities inevitably fostered outbreaks of fatal diseases, and it was usual for those who could afford to do so to retreat to the country until the autumn. In May of 1791, therefore, Elizabeth Hamilton and her children left Philadelphia to join her father, Philip Schuyler, at their family home in Albany, New York.

Shortly before Eliza left the city, Hamilton received a visit at his home from a young woman of twenty-three by the name of Maria Reynolds, who claimed to be in trouble. She told Hamilton that her husband was abusive and unfaithful, and had recently abandoned her to live with another woman.

Maria Reynolds explained that she wished to return to New York to stay with her family, but that she barely had the money to live, let alone make such a long journey. Hamilton, as she may have been aware, had a deeply chivalrous streak and a propensity to come to the defense of women who were destitute, or in danger; Maria Reynolds presented herself as being both. Other men might have been judgmental towards a woman who claimed to have been mistreated by her husband, but Hamilton's childhood had been marred by the abusive actions of his mother's estranged husband, and he tended to give women in similar situations the benefit of the doubt. Hamilton told Reynolds that he would try to gather a little money for her, and would come to visit her at her home later that evening.

The affair that began the evening that Hamilton paid that visit continued for some months while his wife and children remained in Albany, with Hamilton writing to Eliza occasionally, urging her to postpone her return to the city for the sake of her health. Shortly after the affair began, Maria's husband, James Reynolds, made a sudden return to their home; Maria introduced Hamilton to him as someone who had given her financial assistance, and James Reynolds gave the appearance of considering Hamilton a friend. In a pamphlet which he would publish some years later, Hamilton describes how the meetings played out:

"Some time in the summer of the year 1791 a woman called at my house in the city of Philadelphia and asked to speak with me in private. I attended her into a room apart from the family. With a seeming air of affliction she informed that she was a daughter of a Mr. Lewis, sister to a Mr. G. Livingston of the State of New-York, and wife to a Mr. Reynolds whose father was in the Commissary Department during the war with Great Britain, that her husband, who for a long time had treated her very cruelly, had lately left her, to live with another woman, and in so destitute a condition, that though desirous of returning to her friends she had not the means—that knowing I was a citizen of New-York, she had taken the liberty to apply to my humanity for assistance.

"I replied, that her situation was a very interesting one—that I was disposed to afford her assistance to convey her to her friends, but this at the moment not being convenient to me (which was the fact) I must request the place of her residence, to which I should bring or send a small supply of money. She told me the street and the number of the house where she lodged. In the evening I put a bank-bill in my pocket and went to the house. I inquired for Mrs. Reynolds and was shewn up stairs, at the head of which she met me and conducted me into a bed room. I took the bill out of my pocket and gave it to her. Some conversation ensued from which it was quickly apparent that other than pecuniary consolation would be acceptable.

"After this, I had frequent meetings with her, most of them at my own house; Mrs. Hamilton with her children being absent on a visit to her father. In the course of a short time, she mentioned to me that her husband had solicited a reconciliation, and affected to consult me about it. I advised to it, and was soon after informed by her that it had taken place.

"...The intercourse with Mrs. Reynolds, in the mean time, continued; and, though various reflections, (in which a further knowledge of Reynolds' character and the suspicion of some concert between the husband and wife bore a part) induced me to wish a cessation of it; yet her conduct, made it extremely difficult to disentangle myself. All the appearances of violent attachment, and of agonizing distress at the idea of a relinquishment, were played off with a most imposing art. This, though it did not make me entirely the dupe of the plot, yet kept me in a state of irresolution. My sensibility, perhaps my vanity, admitted the possibility of a real fondness; and led me to adopt the plan of a gradual discontinuance rather than of a sudden interruption, as least calculated to give pain, if a real partiality existed."

Before long, Reynolds was extorting money from Hamilton on a regular basis, threatening to write to Eliza if he did not comply, or worse, expose his infidelity to the public in a newspaper. Hamilton suspected that he was being duped from around the point that James Reynolds first entered the picture, but he was never certain in his own mind whether Maria was genuinely in love with him or whether her husband had put her up to seducing him from the beginning.

The truth is probably a mixture of both: Reynolds had married Maria when she was fifteen, and had encouraged or forced her to prostitute herself to other men for his financial benefit in the past. The addition of blackmail was an escalation, possibly prompted by the fact that Hamilton had never been more famous, and while his name was in the newspapers on a daily basis, he was far more approachable than someone like Washington or Jefferson. It must also be admitted that Hamilton had something of a reputation for being, at the very least, a flirt, whose chief pleasure when mingling in society was paying attention to beautiful women.

In any case, he was highly susceptible to Maria Reynolds' advances, and though he claimed to have suspected some form of duplicity early on, he participated in the affair for a considerable length of time—almost a year, all told. And though, eventually, he managed to cut Reynolds off, he was never quite out of his power, as later events would prove.

Chapter Five: Hamilton v. Jefferson

Federalists and Republicans

When the Reynolds affair became public some four years later, it was due in large part to the fact that Jefferson and Madison had grown positively afraid of Hamilton. There was no one else like him on the national stage: he was young, energetic, an expert in a vast array of subjects and disciplines, and vastly popular in the mercantile north. He stood head and shoulders above every other politician with the exception of Washington, and his vision for the country was precisely the opposite of everything that Jefferson and Washington stood for.

They were beginning to suspect that Hamilton stood a good chance of winning a presidential election, should Washington step down, and in their opinion this would be a disaster for the country. It was therefore their duty to organize a unified resistance to Hamilton and his supporters—a task in which they were joined by Aaron Burr, who, though friendly with Hamilton, had abandoned him politically during a recent New York gubernatorial race. The result of this was the creation of the country's first political parties.

Those who subscribed to Hamilton's vision of a strong federal government had long been known as Federalists; anti-Federalists who organized in opposition to them chose to call themselves Republicans, a sly insinuation that Federalists were wealthy aristocrats who were secretly conspiring to convert the new republic into a monarchy.

In modern American politics, the existence of political parties is taken for granted, but in America's infancy, this was not the case. Parties, or factions, were considered a corrupt relic of

British politics. There was as yet no sense that two different visions of government could co-exist without the one dominating and tyrannizing the other. As such, members of both parties saw themselves as the only true and loyal Americans, working to save the new nation from the predations of their opponents. Hamilton, whose Federalist stance was shared by Washington, regarded the formation of an opposition party as borderline treason. Jefferson and Madison, on the other hand, were inveterately loyal to Washington himself, but saw the president as being dangerously under his Treasury secretary's thumb.

Though he was known to be possessed of impeccable judgment and unimpeachable morality, many of Washington's colleagues in government saw him as unsophisticated and unlearned; unlike Jefferson and Madison, who had the wealth and leisure to devote themselves to intense reading and scholarship, Washington had been a surveyor and a soldier and had never attended college. Their belief was that the charismatic, intellectually-dominant, unremittingly verbose Hamilton had secured Washington's personal loyalties during the war, and was now capitalizing on those loyalties by manipulating him into believing whatever Hamilton wanted him to believe. Freed from Hamilton's influence, Jefferson surmised, Washington would be open to persuasion from other quarters. Ironically, this perception of influence hearkened back to the days before the revolution, when American colonists were still proclaiming themselves the loyal subjects of a king who had been duped by his ministers and Parliament into neglecting their interests.

In order to prevent any future possibility of Hamilton becoming president, and hopefully force him from his post as Treasury secretary in the mean time, Jefferson and Madison made a special trip from Philadelphia to New York under the guise of studying the native flora of the mid-Atlantic region. Their real objective was to make inroads into Hamilton's loyal New York base. They knew that voters from the southern states could not block his influence on their own, and that they would need allies from the north. At the same time, Jefferson was amassing a written portfolio of quotations, anecdotes, hearsay, and gossip pertaining to Hamilton—much of it exaggerated, falsified, or simply taken out of context—which became fodder for anonymous attacks in the newspapers, particularly in the *National Gazette,* which was edited by a man named Freneau. (Freneau had been specially recruited by Jefferson to vilify Hamilton in print, though Jefferson insisted that he had hired him only to serve as a translator for the State department. However, as Hamilton pointed out, Freneau was not qualified to translate any language other than French, a language which Jefferson spoke ably.) The enmity between Jefferson and Hamilton grew so heated that Washington asked them both to exercise greater patience with one another. Neither man felt able to comply with this request.

Jefferson attempts to remove Hamilton from office

The backbiting nature of the American political establishment made it virtually inevitable that Hamilton's opponents would eventually get wind of his indiscreet affair with Maria Reynolds and use it against him. Yet exposure first came about through a series of nearly comical coincidences, which culminated in a Jeffersonian loyalist named Jacob Clingman finding himself present at the Reynolds' home during one of Hamilton's visits to Maria.

James and Maria Reynolds were nowhere near being Hamilton's social equals, so the idea that the famous Secretary of the Treasury would have any reason to visit them struck Clingman as exceptionally strange. When he asked James

Reynolds about it, Reynolds smugly insinuated that he knew about all of Hamilton's unsavory business, and that Hamilton had given him money for a scheme involving securities fraud. Clingman and Reynolds were themselves involved in a scheme to defraud the Treasury at the time, and a few years later, they were arrested for it. While Clingman was in prison, he told an undersecretary in the Treasury department that he had information which would implicate Hamilton in corruption.

The information that Reynolds provided was incomplete, but still damning enough of Hamilton that Pennsylvania Congressman Frederick Muhlenberg and Virginia Congressman Abraham Venable took it to James Monroe, seeking advice. Monroe was one of Jefferson's closest allies, and he concluded that they must write to Washington about their suspicions, enclosing the letters Reynolds had supplied them with. First, however, they decided to confront Hamilton in person and give him a chance to explain himself.

Hamilton had been nursing a guilty conscience over his infidelity, and his anxieties had all centered around his wife finding out from a demeaning newspaper essay. On the other hand, it had never occurred to him to be anxious about being accused of securities fraud. He must have felt relieved to find himself facing accusations of something so patently false and easily disproved. Possibly this is why he told his visitors about the affair with Maria Reynolds in grueling personal detail, even to the point of asking them to read letters she and her husband had written him. The letters, at least, proved that Hamilton's secrets were of a personal rather than political nature.

Mollified, the three men promised Hamilton that they would never speak of the matter again. But

Hamilton made a critical error; he allowed James Monroe to take the letters so that they could be copied, and eventually those copies made their way into the hands of Thomas Jefferson.

Jefferson had a history of irrationality where Hamilton was concerned, as evidenced by his conviction, undeviating in the face of all evidence against to the contrary, that Hamilton's secret goal was to convert the republic into a monarchy. Similarly, presented with tantalizing rumors that Hamilton had been implicated in a speculation scheme via his connection to Reynolds, Jefferson chose to believe them, despite the fact that James Monroe had furnished him proofs that Reynolds had only blackmailed him. Jefferson initiated a large scale corruption investigation into Hamilton's conduct as Treasury secretary, first by using a proxy to open inquiries in Congress, then by approaching Washington directly. Washington rebuffed him, however, and the inquiries in Congress served only to exonerate Hamilton on every count.

Midway through Washington's second term, Jefferson was on the verge of resigning his position as Secretary of State. His dogged persecution of Hamilton had caused Washington to lose confidence in his judgment. Washington had begun turning to John Jay for advice on state department matters.

The final breach between Jefferson and Washington came over the matter of American involvement in the war between the newly christened French Republic and Great Britain. Jefferson, an avowed Francophile, had been so much a supporter of the French Revolution that he had coolly approved the execution of Louis XVI and countless others. He considered the United States obligated to ally with France against England, because of the treaties the U.S.

had made with France in return for her aid during the revolution. Hamilton, however, saw that the United States was far too fragile to engage in another war so soon after last. Furthermore, he considered the French Revolution to be an atrocity that would end in despotism, not democracy, and he believed America was not honor-bound to fulfill treaties that had been made with a king whom the present government had guillotined. Washington found Hamilton's argument the more compelling one, and in August of 1793, he issued the nation's first official statement of neutrality, as reproduced below:

"Whereas it appears that a state of war exists between Austria, Prussia, Sardinia, Great Britain, and the United Netherlands, of the one part, and France on the other; and the duty and interest of the United States require, that they should with sincerity and good faith adopt and pursue a conduct friendly and impartial toward the belligerent Powers;

"I have therefore thought fit by these presents to declare the disposition of the United States to observe the conduct aforesaid towards those Powers respectfully; and to exhort and warn the citizens of the United States carefully to avoid all acts and proceedings whatsoever, which may in any manner tend to contravene such disposition.

"And I do hereby also make known, that whatsoever of the citizens of the United States shall render himself liable to punishment or forfeiture under the law of nations, by committing, aiding, or abetting hostilities against any of the said Powers, or by carrying to any of them those articles which are deemed contraband by the modern usage of nations, will not receive the protection of the United States, against such punishment or forfeiture; and further, that I have given instructions to those officers, to whom it belongs, to cause prosecutions to be instituted against all persons, who shall, within the cognizance of the courts of the United States, violate the law of nations, with respect to the Powers at war, or any of them."

Thomas Jefferson, no longer able to tolerate his lack of influence with Washington, resigned on December 31, 1793.

The Whiskey Rebellion

One of Hamilton's duties as Treasury secretary was to levy and collect taxes, which were necessary to give the federal government a stream of revenue. Hamilton had come up with the idea to impose a federal tax on whiskey and hard liquors when he was writing the Federalist Papers years earlier, and now, presented with a choice between levying a domestic tax and raising the import tariffs on goods from Europe (which Hamilton knew from experience would encourage an increase in smuggling) Hamilton chose to impose an excise task on whiskey. This shortly gave rise to the most serious threat to the stability of the American government since the British were expelled: an uprising of farmers from the mountainous western regions of Pennsylvania, in what became known as the Whiskey Rebellion.

The problem, as far as the Pennsylvanians were concerned, was that the whiskey tax had a more severe effect on them than on anyone else in the country, and they were already very poor to begin with. They were wheat farmers, and their crop grew in plentiful abundance, but they couldn't transport it east for sale in large amounts because travel through the mountain range was slow and perilous. By making whiskey from it, they got a product that could be stored for long periods of time and transported conveniently, or else used in place of commerce within the community. Because the western Pennsylvania economy was so dependent on whiskey, the tax roused bitter memories of the British taxes that had sparked the revolution, and a large number of Pennsylvanians decided that rebellion was, again, the best response.

By the winter of 1794, the spirit of the French Revolution had infected American patriots to such a degree that it led to the formation of "Republican" societies, in which the members addressed one another by the title of "Citizen", just as in the French Republic. Hamilton, who was disgusted by the French Revolution, was already fearful that the fashion for rebellion would lead to unrest in America, and he blamed the uprising in Pennsylvania on French influence. He urged Washington to answer the revolt swiftly, and with a display of great force. It was Hamilton's belief that if the government responded with overwhelming numbers, it would not actually have to use them; the rebels would disperse and go home, and the authority of the new government, answering the first real challenge to its authority since winning independence, would prove that rebellion was not to be tolerated.

Washington agreed with Hamilton, and actually put the responsibility for managing the response to the rebellion chiefly in his hands. This ought to have been the purview of Henry Knox, who was Secretary of War, but he chose to withdraw at the beginning of the crisis on the pretext of seeing to a property dispute. Hamilton and Washington traveled to Pennsylvania at the head of a muster of 12,000 militia, and Hamilton, just as at home in a military camp now as he had been during the revolution, personally inspected the troops, managed the arrival and distribution of supplies and equipment, and even took over guard duty shift from a lax sentinel who complained that it was too difficult to remain on his feet the whole time.

Hamilton's plan to overwhelm the rebels with a display of superior force proved effective, and the uprising was dispersed without any open hostilities. Washington, who dreaded the prospect of using federal firepower against domestic unrest, had given his word that none of his men would fire on the rebels unless they were fired upon first, and he kept that promise. In the end, some one hundred and fifty rebels were arrested, mostly for violent acts committed against civilians, and when two of Washington's men were found to have killed civilians, they were turned over to civilian courts to be tried, thus proving that martial law had not been enacted.

Hamilton's conclusion was that the nation was in dire need of a professional "standing" army, one that remained in training even when the nation was not at war. This was yet another point on which he clashed with Jefferson and Madison, who knew that the existence of a standing army would give the federal government even more power. There was little Jefferson could do immediately, however, as he had resigned from Washington's cabinet the previous year, giving up his position as Secretary of State to Edmund Randolph, the former attorney general. But Jefferson took careful note of the resentment that Hamilton's whiskey tax had created, and when he was elected president six years later, he was bolstered to a large extent by the votes he garnered by promising to abolish it.

Hamilton After Washington

In January of 1795, shortly after his fortieth birthday, Hamilton resigned as George Washington's Secretary of the Treasury. Rather than being forced out of office, as Jefferson had hoped, he left of his own accord, and made a point of giving Congress prior notice of his departure, in case there were any more inquiries into his professional conduct they wished to make before he could no longer be held accountable. That winter, Elizabeth Hamilton and their fourth oldest child were recovering from a serious illness; furthermore, Elizabeth had recently miscarried a pregnancy. Hamilton had been working his fingers to the bone since the end of the war, and he was past ready to spend time at home with his family.

Hamilton's enemies were fond of supposing that he was secretly a millionaire, or at least that he had hundreds of thousands of pounds secreted away in the British banks he admired so much. Jefferson himself was so convinced that Hamilton had enriched himself with unethical gains from the Treasury department that he openly sneered at a newspaper report indicating that Hamilton had left Washington's cabinet because he urgently needed to resume his law practice for financial reasons. The latter report was accurate, however; Hamilton had never taken a penny from unethical dealings, and he made far less money as Secretary of the Treasury than he had as a lawyer. He had been forced to go into debt just to support his family, which seemed to increase in size every year. Hamilton's enemies seemed to find it impossible to believe that the man who had created the American securities market had not found a way to make a private profit off of his public duty. But Hamilton was strictly conscientious about avoiding even the appearance of corruption; this preoccupation with his personal honor, though one of his more admirable traits, would lead to dire consequences in the future.

Rejoining his family in Albany, Hamilton sequestered himself from politics for a short time; inevitably, however, politics came to find him. Shortly after Hamilton's resignation from the cabinet, John Jay traveled to England for talks with the British regarding the treaties which had been agreed to as part of the peace settlement at the end of the war. Among other things, the Americans wanted the British to return the slaves who had taken advantage of the British offer of freedom in exchange for abandoning their colonial masters. They also wanted the British to surrender their fortifications in the northwest, and stop seizing American ships on the pretext of keeping them from falling into French hands.

The concessions which Jay was able to get from the British were more generous, as Hamilton pointed out, than those Britain had conceded to any other nation, but they still did not satisfy Americans at home. The treaty was unpopular with nearly everyone, but the Jeffersonians adopted it as a special proof that the Federalists had been in bed with the British all along. Though Hamilton did not work for Washington anymore, Washington wrote to him and asked for his opinion about the treaty, specifically, whether the concessions were adequate, and whether he should sign it. Hamilton promptly dropped his law practice for a few days and wrote yet another of his trademark lengthy, closely reasoned, brilliantly argued treatises, examining the Jay treaty in minute detail, and offering the ultimate opinion that while, some parts of it could be better, it was on the whole a good deal for the nation.

When Washington signed the treaty, there was massive public outrage, including public debates that sometimes turned into riots. Hamilton personally challenged one man to a duel, and received a challenge from another; both were offended by his defense of the Jay treaty. Hamilton accepted the duels, but managed to negotiate them both to a peace before the fights could take place. He continued to defend the treaty, both in debate and in print, publishing a series of newspaper essays in July of 1795 under the name of "Camillus". An excerpt from the first of the Camillus essays appears below:

"It is only to consult the history of nations to perceive, that every country, at all times, is cursed by the existence of men, who, actuated by an irregular ambition, scruple nothing which they imagine will contribute to their own advancement and importance. In monarchies, supple courtiers; in republics, fawning or turbulent demagogues, worshipping still the idol power wherever placed, whether in the hands of a prince, or of the people, and trafficking in the weaknesses, vices, frailties, or prejudices of the one or the other. It was to have been expected, that such men, counting more on the passions than on the reason of their fellow citizens, and anticipating that the treaty would have to struggle with prejudices, would be disposed to make an alliance with popular discontent, to nourish it, and to press it into the service of their particular views.

"It was not to have been doubted, that there would be one or more foreign powers, indisposed to a measure which accommodated our differences with Great Britain, and laid the foundation of future good understanding, merely because it had that effect.

"Nations are never content to confine their rivalships and enmities to themselves. It is their usual policy to disseminate them as widely, as they can, regardless how far it may interfere with the tranquility or happiness of the nations which they are able to influence. Whatever pretentions may be made, the world is yet remote from the spectacle of that just and generous policy, whether in the cabinets of republics or of kings, which would dispose one nation, in its intercourses with another; satisfied with a due proportion of privileges and benefits to see that other pursue freely, its true interest, with regard to a third; though at the expence of no engagement, nor in violation of any rule of friendly or fair procedure. It was natural that the contrary spirit should produce efforts of foreign counteraction to the treaty, and it was certain that the partizans of the counteracting power would second its efforts by all the means which they thought calculated to answer the end."

Thomas Jefferson, naturally, was an ardent opponent of the Jay Treaty, but he was suffering from poor health at the time, and did not attempt to challenge it personally. Instead, he asked Madison, who often took up his pen to voice Jefferson's opinions, to write a reply to the Camillus essays. Madison declined, but he did lend his support in Congress to a reactionary measure that proposed to reserve the power of approving future treaties to Congress, rather than to the president. The measure failed, but Washington took Madison's support for it as a personal insult. Washington had always considered Madison a friend, and had long relied on his advice in matters pertaining to Constitutional law. Here at the latter end of Washington's presidency, however, Madison and Jefferson were both losing his trust and friendship. Madison, in particular, never spoke to Washington in private again after the affair of the Jay treaty.

Washington's Farewell Address

Washington's decision to step down from the presidency after the conclusion of his second term in office stunned the world no less than his resigning from the head of the army after the end of the war had done. Though it is now Constitutional law that American presidents may serve no more than two terms, this was, until the 1950's, merely a matter of tradition and precedent, a precedent that had been set by Washington. He probably would have had no difficulty in being elected to a third term, but Washington had grown exhausted during his last few years in office, subjected as he was to endless criticism in the newspapers from Jeffersonian essayists. He longed to return to Mount Vernon and spend what remained of his life in pastoral retreat. Therefore, towards the end of 1795, Washington turned to Hamilton, whose skill with the pen dwarfed that of any other person of Washington's acquaintance, and asked him to look over a draft of the farewell address that Madison had written for him towards the end of his first term, before Washington made up his mind to run again.

Hamilton expounded eloquently upon Madison's words and Washington's ideas, and ended up producing one of the most enduring and memorable documents in American state history. The last paragraphs in particular exhibits the graceful turns of phrase which were Hamilton's stock in trade as a writer; they are reproduced here in the following excerpt:

"In offering to you, my countrymen, these counsels of an old and affectionate friend, I dare not hope they will make the strong and lasting impression I could wish; that they will control the usual current of the passions, or prevent our nation from running the course which has hitherto marked the destiny of nations. But, if I may even flatter myself that they may be productive of some partial benefit, some occasional good; that they may now and then recur to moderate the fury of party spirit, to warn against the mischiefs of foreign intrigue, to guard against the impostures of pretended patriotism; this hope will be a full recompense for the solicitude for your welfare, by which they have been dictated[...]

"Though, in reviewing the incidents of my administration, I am unconscious of intentional error, I am nevertheless too sensible of my defects not to think it probable that I may have committed many errors. Whatever they may be, I fervently beseech the Almighty to avert or mitigate the evils to which they may tend. I shall also carry with me the hope that my country will never cease to view them with indulgence; and that, after forty five years of my life dedicated to its service with an upright zeal, the faults of incompetent abilities will be consigned to oblivion, as myself must soon be to the mansions of rest."

The speech also contains Washington's stern admonition against allowing political parties and factions to become a threat to the unity of the people and government. The destructive lengths that his countrymen would go to in order to further the interests of their parties was one of the bitterest lessons Washington had learned in his second term. Ironically, the Jeffersonian portion of Washington's audience were so incensed by the speech that the fission between them and their Federalist counterparts only widened.

Chapter Six: Hamilton v. Adams

The Election of 1796

Hamilton was inarguably the second most powerful man in the country during Washington's presidency. Even after he resigned his post as Treasury secretary, he exerted an influence over Washington and over public policy rivaled by no one else. After his resignation, though playing no official role in politics, he remained one of the Federalist elites, whose influence and say-so would determine the party's future, including who it would field as a presidential candidate during the election of 1796.

Hamilton was not interested in obtaining the presidency for himself, though some members of his party encouraged him to run. He was, at the time, still a bit younger than most of his colleagues, and according to Hamilton's way of thinking, there were too many qualified men of the older generation entitled to be considered before him for him to consider running yet. Furthermore, Hamilton biographer Ron Chernow theorizes that Hamilton lacked the temperament to be a leader, saying: "His conception of leadership was noble but limiting: the true statesman defied the wishes of the people, if necessary, and shook them from wishful thinking and complacency. Hamilton lived in a world of moral absolutes and was not especially prone to compromise or consensus building." He also had to consider the possibility that his political enemies had got hold of his letters from Maria Reynolds and might blackmail him or expose him if he entered the race.

Hamilton's goal as a Federalist party leader during the 1796 election was quite simple: stop Thomas Jefferson from becoming president by any means possible. This led him to support South Carolinian Thomas Pinckney as the

Federalist candidate. Only a southerner, he surmised, capable of dividing the southern bloc of voters, would have a chance of defeating Jefferson. Vice-President John Adams, however, was understood to be the prevailing Federalist favorite, and Hamilton's attempts to get Pinckney elected ahead of him were seen as underhanded, backbiting behavior—especially by Adams, who promptly added a Federalist voice to the throng of Jeffersonian Republicans railing against Hamilton in anonymous newspaper essays.

Ultimately, Adams won the election with seventy-one votes, while Jefferson was elected just behind him as vice-president with sixty eight votes. Jefferson and Adams were of opposite political parties, but they had once been friends, and now their friendship was renewed over their mutual dislike of Hamilton. Hamilton and Adams had similar views on many political issues, but Adams was rather vain and prone to grudges, and he had resented Hamilton ever since Washington had elevated him to a position of influence on his staff. Though Adams retained Washington's cabinet, rather than making entirely new appointments, he did not avail himself of the advice of Washington's chief advisor, even though Hamilton lost no time after Adams' election in drafting him a long letter full of the same sort of advice he had once given Washington.

The Reynolds Pamphlet

In 1797, Hamilton's sister in law, Angelica Church, came back to live in the United States after a decade or so of living in London while her husband served as a member of Parliament. The Churches made a considerable impact on the staid New York society to which they returned; Angelica showcased the newest fashions from Europe, and her husband John kept to his dissolute European habits of hosting gambling parties that lasted into the wee hours of the morning. As to Hamilton, there soon sprang up a rumor in Republican papers that he and Angelica were having an affair. Imprecations of "incest" (an allusion to Angelica being Hamilton's sister-in-law) and adultery began to appear in the newspapers that routinely dragged Hamilton's name through the mud.

In the summer of 1797, a pamphlet, written by James Thomson Callender, printed a version of the same rumor that had sent James Monroe and three colleagues to Hamilton's home some four years earlier, on the verge of exposing evidence of his supposed speculations to Washington. Callender had managed, probably though carelessness or deliberate malice on Monroe's part, to get hold of the letters between Hamilton and Maria and James Reynolds. He printed them in his paper as proof that Hamilton had given Reynolds money for his illegal financial schemes.

Hamilton's adultery was exposed, but it did not exonerate him from the charge of corruption, as he had hoped: "Such correspondence could not refer exclusively to wenching," Callender wrote, referring to the many letters James Reynolds had written to Hamilton demanding money. Monroe, Muhlenberg, and Venable had accepted Hamilton account of the blackmail as an adequate explanation for Reynolds's correspondence, but Callender seemed to find the idea of a man as powerful as Hamilton allowing himself to fall into the power of a petty blackmailer absurd. That they had been conspiring together for mutual profit seemed a far more likely story.

Hamilton chose to answer Callender's accusations as he had answered every other challenge made to him in his career: by writing an exceptionally long, overly detailed essay that rebutted the charges against him point by point. Acting on the principle that if he admitted to being guilty of a misstep in his private life, he could prove that he had not jeopardized the honor of his public office, he laid bare every aspect of his adulterous affair with Maria Reynolds and James Reynolds' attempt to blackmail him. The following long excerpt demonstrates the uncomfortable degree of detail Hamilton was willing to reveal to the public to prove that, even if he had been unfaithful, he had not been dishonest:

"I owe perhaps to my friends an apology for condescending to give a public explanation. A just pride with reluctance stoops to a formal vindication against so despicable a contrivance and is inclined rather to oppose to it the uniform evidence of an upright character. This would be my conduct on the present occasion, did not the tale seem to derive a sanction from the names of three men16 of some weight and consequence in the society: a circumstance, which I trust will excuse me for paying attention to a slander that without this prop, would defeat itself by intrinsic circumstances of absurdity and malice.

"The charge against me is a connection with one James Reynolds for purposes of improper pecuniary speculation. My real crime is an amorous connection with his wife, for a considerable time with his privity and connivance, if not originally brought on by a combination between the husband and wife with the design to extort money from me.

"This confession is not made without a blush. I cannot be the apologist of any vice because the ardour of passion may have made it mine. I can never cease to condemn myself for the pang, which it may inflict in a bosom eminently intitled to all my gratitude, fidelity and love. But that bosom will approve, that even at so great an expence, I should effectually wipe away a more serious stain from a name, which it cherishes with no less elevation than tenderness. The public too will I trust excuse the confession. The necessity of it to my defence against a more heinous charge could alone have extorted from me so painful an indecorum."

This essay (entitled "Observations on Certain Documents Contained in No. V & VI of "The History of the United States for the Year 1796," In Which the Charge of Speculation Against Alexander Hamilton, Late Secretary of the Treasury, Is Fully Refuted. Written by Himself" and known informally as "the Reynolds Pamphlet") had an unfortunate effect on Hamilton's political career. It provided a foundation for salacious rumors about his character that have persisted into the historical record.

Both Alexander and Eliza Hamilton blamed James Monroe for the affair coming to light, for two reasons: the first was that Monroe had, after confronting Hamilton in 1793, sworn to keep the matter a secret, and he had betrayed that promise by giving Hamilton's letters to his clerk to be copied. The second was that Monroe failed to correct Hamilton's enemies when they asserted that he, Muhlenberg, and Venable had not been satisfied as to Hamilton's innocence when they confronted him privately. Hamilton wrote to Monroe, insisting that he set the record straight, and when Monroe did not immediately answer him, Hamilton went to see him personally. The meeting nearly ended in a duel. (Eliza Hamilton would probably have dueled him if she could; Monroe attempted to apologize to her when she was an elderly widow, but she never forgave him.)

Ironically, the duel between Monroe and Hamilton was probably only avoided thanks to the intercession of Aaron Burr, who advised Monroe that he was in the wrong for not publically admitting Hamilton's innocence. Burr was still a friend to Hamilton at this point; that would change before the century's end.

The XYZ Affair and the Quasi-War

After having narrowly avoided a second war with Britain during the affair of Jay's Treaty, America seemed poised for war with France for a long time following the so-called XYZ affair—named for the pseudonymous initials given to three French ministers who attempted to extort bribes from American diplomatic officials who had come to discuss the French seizure of American merchant vessels in neutral waters. When news of the attempted extortion reached the United States, there was enormous political tumult: not only did the betrayal rankle coming from such a close ally, but any hint of misconduct on the part of the French was immediately laid to the account of the Jeffersonian Republicans, who were as sentimental about France as the Federalists were accused of being about England. Federalists, accordingly, swept the next round of Congressional elections, though their dominance would only last until the next presidential election.

Diplomacy with France having failed in a spectacular manner, many Americans were calling for war. During the Whiskey Rebellion, Hamilton had called for the formation of a standing army; now, at last, Congress authorized the creation of a Department of the Navy and an army of 10,000 men, plus twelve infantry regiments and six cavalry companies.

The question of who should manage the army was more complicated: by Constitutional law, the president was the commander in chief, but Washington was a soldier and had led the American army during the revolution. Adams, by contrast, had read some military theory, but he had never been on a battlefield. Adams had always been somewhat jealous of Washington's reputation and stature, but now he turned command of America's armies back over to the former president without hesitation (and without even asking first whether Washington was *willing* to take command.)

Washington accepted control of the army, but at the age of sixty-three, he could no longer ride long days on horseback. Only if a war was actually declared was Washington willing to become directly involved, and then only to legitimize the exercise by his presence. Until then, he required a younger, more active man to be his second-in-command. Washington informed Adams that he could only accept command of the army if either Hamilton or Charles Cotesworth Pinckney were his second; he also provided Adams with the names of those whom he wished to be appointed as his generals. Adams was outraged; he felt that as commander-in-chief it was his privilege to name generals. In the end, however, he felt compelled to accept Washington's decision.

This was Hamilton's first foray back into a life of public service since publishing the pamphlet about his affair with Maria Reynolds, and Republicans made much of the fact that "the same Hamilton who published a book to prove that he is AN ADULTERER" had been given such an important post. Nevertheless, he went from being addressed as "Colonel Hamilton" to being addressed as "General Hamilton"; his official rank was Inspector General, roughly equivalent to that of a major general. It was his task to organize the American army, down to the composition of battalions, the design of uniforms, and the maintenance of supply lines. His aide-de-camp was his nephew, Philip Church, Angelica Church's son, and he relied on his nephew as Washington had relied on him in the war. In fact, Hamilton threw himself into the role of general with such vigor that Abigail Adams, not entirely meaning to pay him a compliment, called him "Little Mars".

The Manhattan Company

In the summer of 1798, another epidemic of
yellow fever swept the city of New York, and
infection was rampant in Manhattan that
approximately forty-five people were dying every
day. At the time, the sources of the disease were
not perfectly understood, but it was accepted
that contaminated water played a large role in
spreading the disease. Once again, everyone who
could afford to flee the city did so, and while
Eliza Hamilton threw herself into working for a
charitable society to meet the needs of widows
and orphans left destitute by the disease,
Alexander Hamilton was enlisted by Aaron Burr
in a scheme to prevent future outbreaks.

Though Burr had always been a Republican, he
gave the appearance of moderation and
reasonableness by keeping his opinions to
himself whenever possible. He had run for vice

president against John Adams in the election of 1796 and was now a member of the New York General Assembly. For a few years after, particularly since the XYZ affair, he gave Hamilton the impression that he was considering changing parties and becoming a Federalist. It was for this reason, possibly, that Hamilton was eager to help him when Burr asked for his help in approaching the mayor of New York for a charter to create a water company—one that would lay down pipes and create sewers and pump clean water into the city, to replace the contaminated wells that led to the yellow fever epidemics. This purported water company was known as the Manhattan Company.

Unsuspected by Hamilton, Burr's real aim was to exploit a loophole in the wording of the Manhattan Company's charter that permitted nothing less than the formation of an unofficial bank. Up to that point, there were only two banks in New York: Hamilton had helped create both of them and both of them were under Federalist control, to the point that Republicans claimed that if they expressed an anti-Federalist opinion in public or in print, their requests for loans would be denied. Far from being on the point of changing political parties, Burr wanted to start what would effectively be the first Republican-controlled bank in the city. Plenty of Republicans were inherently suspicious of banks, but many would welcome the opportunity to use one that didn't require them to get into bed with their political enemies.

Hamilton was infuriated when he realized how Burr had used him. Once the company had received its charter, it abandoned all pretense of providing the city with clean water, instead laying in a pipe system that transported the contaminated well water around the city. This incident perhaps marked the turning point in Hamilton's relationship with Burr; friendly despite their political differences, the most famous duel in American history lay in their future, and only one of them would survive it.

The Death of George Washington

By 1799, Adams had elected to send a peace delegation to France, a decision he undertook without bothering to inform or consult Hamilton, despite the fact that he was in the process of organizing the American military in preparation for a war with that country. Hamilton, outraged, sought Adams out for a private discussion on the subject; when the conversation was over, Hamilton departed, never to speak privately with Adams again.

He had been the most important and indispensable of all Washington's advisors, but Adams's personal dislike of Hamilton was extreme, and he was incapable of profiting from any advice that Hamilton gave him. Hamilton did not react well to being excluded in this manner. Though Adams professed not to know it, his entire cabinet was corresponding with Hamilton and getting advice from him on a weekly basis, much of it passed on to Adams without attribution in the form of memos. It no doubt rankled Hamilton to bear so much responsibility for steering the ship of state while receiving no credit for his efforts.

George Washington, however, had always seen the wisdom in Hamilton's advice, and had always recognized the scope of his extraordinary talents. Though as a young man Hamilton had felt that Washington stood in the way of his pursuit of battlefield glory, their relationship was now easy and affectionate. Washington embraced Hamilton as a peer and Hamilton saw how much he owed to the fact that Washington had always had faith in his abilities. Even his personal failings had been met with an indulgent eye by his old mentor; after the affair with Maria

Reynolds came out in the newspapers, Washington had sent the Hamiltons an expensive present in the form of a silver wine cooler with four cups.

Washington died, suddenly, in late December of 1799, of a throat infection which he contracted after riding for miles in the rain when he already had a cold. His final letter to Hamilton, on the subject of establishing an American military academy, was the last letter he ever wrote. Hamilton was both personally despondent and professionally dismayed by Washington's death; harried by enemies and detractors, Hamilton knew how much he would miss the protection that Washington's quiet presence in the political background had afforded him. And in fact, Adams lost no time in making Hamilton as irrelevant as possible: by the spring of 1800, Napoleon was the dictator of France, America was pursuing a French peace, and the army that Hamilton had poured all his energy into creating was disbanded without firing a shot at an enemy. Hamilton resigned his commission and returned to practicing law in New York.

In the years after leaving Washington's cabinet, there were one or two incidents in which Hamilton displayed poor judgment, uncharacteristic of him—something which Chernow attributes to his being separated from Washington's influence. While the two men had similar philosophies of government and goals for the nation's future, they had markedly different temperaments. Washington was, like Hamilton, a person of strong feeling and quick temper, but he had taught himself exemplary restraint and self-control in his youth. Hamilton, on the other hand, while not prone to irrational outbursts, took any perceived slight to his honor deeply to heart—and as he had tied his personal honor to the fate of the American government, the political was very much personal with him. When he had served Washington, first as his aide-de-camp, then as his Treasury Secretary, some of Washington's restraint had governed him. Now that Washington was gone, there was no longer anyone close enough to Hamilton, with enough understanding of his personality, to exercise that sort of influence over him.

The New York regional election which took place in the spring of 1800 was a disaster for the Federalist party and presaged Adams's defeat by Jefferson in the presidential election shortly to follow. It also featured the first instances of open electioneering in American political history, as Aaron Burr began canvassing support for his next bid for the vice-presidency. American politicians had never campaigned for office before—it had always been the style for a potential president or congressmen to pretend to be indifferent and lacking in all ambition, while his supporters drummed up votes on his behalf. Burr however was openly soliciting the support of his fellow New Yorkers, possibly because he had lost his seat in the General Assembly over the Manhattan Company affair.

Burr formed an alliance of New York Republicans and Virginia Jeffersonians, and the Republican sweep of New York that resulted was something like Hamilton's worst nightmare. In a desperate attempt to prevent the Republicans from taking power, Hamilton asked Governor John Jay to alter the rules governing elections, switching from a representative voting system to one featuring direct popular elections. Furthermore—an example of the poor judgment he was sometimes prone to after Washington— Hamilton asked Jay to apply the rules retroactively to the election that had just taken place. Jay refused, feeling, quite understandably, that this uncharacteristically underhanded bid to overturn the results of a democratic election were beneath both Hamilton and himself.

Pamphlet on John Adams

In May of 1800, having seen the disastrous anti-Federalist sweep of the regional elections, and anticipating that his chances at re-election were growing weaker, John Adams conducted a sudden and shocking "purge" of his cabinet, firing all three of his departmental secretaries on the grounds that they had been partly selected by Hamilton during Washington's presidency. He claimed to have recently discovered that Hamilton was writing to his staff members, who were presenting his advice to Adams as their own; some historians think it more likely that Adams was hoping to curry Republican favor and votes by firing the High Federalists in his cabinet. The truth may be somewhere in the middle. Adams was definitely concerned that he wouldn't be re-elected, and he was also furious with Hamilton in a way that made his former irritability seem like fond affection.

Throughout his political life, Hamilton had a tendency to think that the worst was likely to happen during elections, and he threw himself into heading off those worst case scenarios in a way that at times seemed paranoid. In the election of 1800, he was convinced that Adams could not beat Jefferson for president, and therefore he attempted to persuade key Federalists in New England (which was Adams's home territory) to vote for Charles Cotesworth Pinckney, a South Carolinian, instead. Adams had probably got wind of this by the time he fired Secretary of War James McHenry, because Adams accused him directly of conspiring against him with Hamilton. Adams went on to make comments about Hamilton's illegitimate birth and his being a "foreigner" from the West Indies—comments that McHenry eventually relayed to Hamilton. Close-mouthed and sensitive on the topic of his birth and childhood as he was on no other subject, Hamilton was deeply wounded by Adams's remarks, and he was outraged over the manner in which Adams had treated McHenry and his colleagues.

Suddenly, the prospect of Adams continuing as president for another four years seemed to Hamilton even more disastrous than the idea of Jefferson being elected president. He abandoned his hopes of having Pinckney win first place and Adams second in the voting tally; he now hoped for a Pinckney victory and a Jefferson vice-presidency. To bring this about, Hamilton did what he always did when he wanted to provoke change in the political landscape: he wrote a treatise.

Everyone who had worked with Adams during his presidency was of the opinion that he was dangerously unstable, prone to fits of passion and temper that were deeply unsuitable in a head of state. After Adams fired his cabinet, Hamilton consulted with McHenry and came to the conclusion that other high ranking members of the Federalist party needed to be made aware that the incumbent president was not fit for re-election. The essay which Hamilton produced on the subject was meant for private circulation, not publication; but someone who got hold of it passed it on to the Republican newspaper, the *Aurora*, which printed excerpts of it. Feeling that it was better to publish the entire document than to let people read only the parts of it that his political opponents saw fit to show them, Hamilton printed the entire letter as a pamphlet entitled "Concerning the Public Conduct and Character of John Adams, Esq., President of the United States", an excerpt of which appears below. In the excerpt, Hamilton complains scathingly of Adams's approach to foreign policy with France:

"The latter conduct of the President forms a painful contrast to his commencement. Its effects have been directly the reverse. It has sunk the tone of the public mind—it has impaired the confidence of the friends of the Government in the Executive Chief—it has distracted public opinion—it has unnerved the public councils—it has sown the seeds of discord at home, and lowered the reputation of the Government abroad. The circumstances which preceded, aggravate the disagreeableness of the results. They prove that the injudicious things which have been acted, were not the effects of any regular plan, but the fortuitous emanations of momentary impulses.

"The session, which ensued the promulgation of the dispatches of our Commissioners, was about to commence. Mr. Adams arrived at Philadelphia from his seat at Quincy. The tone of his mind seemed to have been raised, rather than depressed.

"It was suggested to him, that it might be expedient to insert in his Speech of Congress, a sentiment of this import: That after the repeatedly rejected advances of this country, its dignity required that it should be left with France in future to make the first overture; that if, desirous of reconciliation, she should evince the disposition by sending a Minister to this Government, he would be received with the respect due to his character, and treated with in the frankness of a sincere desire of accommodation.

"The suggestion was received in a manner both indignant and intemperate.

"Mr. Adams declared as a sentiment which he had adopted on mature reflection: That if France should send a Minister to-morrow, he would order him back the day after.

"So imprudent an idea was easily refuted. Little argument was requisite to shew that by a similar system of retaliation, when one Government in a particular instance had refused the Envoy of another, nations might entail upon each other perpetual hostility; mutually barring the avenues of explanation.

"In less than forty-eight hours from this extraordinary sally, the mind of Mr. Adams underwent a total revolution—he resolved not only to insert in his speech the sentiment which had been proposed to him, but to go farther, and to declare, that if France would give explicit assurances of receiving a Minister from this country, with due respect, he would send one.

"In vain was this extension of the sentiment opposed by all his Ministers, as being equally incompatible with good policy, and with the dignity of the nation—he obstinately persisted, and the pernicious declaration was introduced."

Publishing the pamphlet spelled instant disaster for the Federalist party, and for Hamilton's political career. As Chernow puts it: "In 'The Reynolds Pamphlet', Hamilton had exposed only his own folly. In the Adams pamphlet, he displayed both his own errant judgment *and* Adams's instability." Jefferson would go on to tie in the presidential election with Aaron Burr, while Adams came in ahead of Pinckney by just one vote.

The Election of 1800

The question of how to break the deadlock between Jefferson and Burr weighed heavily on Hamilton's mind. He was no longer occupying any official office, and his credibility had been greatly damaged after publishing his pamphlet on Adams. Nonetheless, his opinion weighed heavily with many Federalists, and he felt obligated to influence events to the best of his wisdom. As much as he had always disliked Jefferson, Hamilton found the prospect of a Burr presidency deeply alarming. He gave his opinion of Burr frankly to his longtime colleague, Oliver Wolcott, saying that,

"As to *Burr*, there is nothing in his favour. His private character is not defended by his most partial friends. He is bankrupt beyond redemption, except by the plunder of his country. His public principles have no other spring or aim than his own aggrandizement.... If he can, he will certainly disturb our institutions to secure to himself *permanent power* and with it *wealth.*"

It seems likely that the affair of the Manhattan Company was weighing heavily on Hamilton's mind when he made this assertion.

As to Jefferson, Hamilton was prepared to concede that, if he attained the presidency, he might do less damage than his opinions would seem to indicate. For instance, as much as Jefferson had railed against the authority of a powerful central government, Hamilton doubted that Jefferson would take any measures to reduce executive privilege while he himself was the executive wielding them. Compared to Burr,

Jefferson was more intelligent, talented, and capable; and, as Chernow puts it, "Hamilton preferred a man with wrong principles to one devoid of any."

The degree to which Hamilton was responsible for the deadlock actually breaking in Jefferson's favor is debatable. He had published a pamphlet and lost Adams a certain number of votes, weakening the Federalist base in New York enough to give Burr a foothold. The initial vote took place in the Senate, which in the event of ties, sent the ballot to the House of Representatives, where a simple majority of nine out of the sixteen states would decide the outcome of the election. The House could not seem to muster nine whole votes for either candidate, however, and had to put the ballot to the vote dozens of times.

It was still considered gauche for candidates to campaign openly, and it seems that Burr remained in New York minding his own business during the House deliberations. Jefferson, however, lived not far away from the newly constructed capital of Washington City, and he made a point of being available to answer any questions the voting Congressmen might have had about what sort of president he intended to be. Meanwhile, Hamilton was furiously writing letters to influential Congressmen, particularly James Bayard of Delaware, who was the sole representative of his state. (All states cast their votes according to the consensus of their delegations, which meant that there were generally one or two abstentions from states where the delegates could not agree. As there was only one delegate from Delaware, however, his sole vote swayed the electoral ballot of the whole state.)

Bayard was a Federalist, but most Federalists, having hated Jefferson for so long, were inclined to vote for Burr. Hamilton managed to talk Bayard around to an abstention, however, and when both Virginia and Maryland abstained as well, Jefferson emerged with a ten vote majority as the duly elected president. John Adams, weary after a long, embattled term of office, and grieving the recent death of his younger son, chose not to attend Jefferson's inauguration, making him one of only three outgoing presidents in American history to snub their successors in this way.

Chapter Seven: Hamilton At Home

The Death of Philip Hamilton

There was little left for Hamilton to do after Thomas Jefferson took office as the third president of the United States. Jefferson systematically excluded all Federalists from positions of any significance in the government. (He also excluded Vice-President Aaron Burr from all decision-making, driving Burr to shore up support from amongst disaffected Federalists and so-called "Old Republicans" who were dismayed by the moderate turn Jefferson took once he was in power.) Hamilton had been on the front lines of American history almost since the day he had arrived in the country as a teenager; now, at the age of forty-six, he was entirely on the outskirts of power.

Fortunately, Hamilton had a wife he was still passionately fond of and seven children upon whom he doted to fill the time that was no longer consumed by politics. He also had family coffers that were badly in need of replenishing, and a reputation as the most brilliant lawyer in New York to support him. For years, he and Eliza had spent as much time together as they could, but the span in their children's ages necessitated that the little ones remain with Eliza for about half the year while the elder children stayed with Alexander in town. Now, no such division was necessary. Hamilton set about building a modest but beautiful seven bedroom home for his family on a plot of land a few miles outside Manhattan, and in the time left over from his law practice he threw himself into designing the grounds and gardens. In some ways, it must have been bewildering and dissatisfying for Hamilton to be exiled from the seat of power; on the other hand, he seemed to throw himself into the business of being a father and a husband with touching enthusiasm and sincerity.

In 1801, the Hamilton children, in order of age, were Philip, nineteen years old; Angelica, seventeen; Alexander, fifteen; James, thirteen; John, nine; William, four; and Eliza, two. The eighth and final child would be born in 1802, but there would only ever be seven young Hamiltons at a time. The youngest son was named Philip in honor of his oldest brother, who died in a duel six months before he was born.

Philip Hamilton was an exceptionally handsome and talented young man by all accounts, and Hamilton set great store by his prospects. He had many of his father's traits, including intelligence, eloquence, and a tendency to throw himself headlong into frays. In 1801, a man about ten year Philip's senior named George Eacker gave a speech, later printed in the papers, which blamed Hamilton for the Quasi-War with France and levied criticism against his handling of the army. A few months later, in November, Philip Hamilton and a friend spotted Eacker at a play and entered his theater box to force a confrontation with him over the speech. Eacker was so offended by their behavior (which even Hamilton later admitted had probably put Philip in the wrong) that he demanded a duel with both of them, and they both accepted.

Philip consulted his father before the duel took place, and Hamilton advised him to fire his pistol at the sky when the time came, according to a French custom which existed to satisfy affairs of honor without bloodshed. Hamilton had certainly not hesitated to throw himself into duels when he was younger, but time had taught him to think differently of such matters; he had become more religious in his retirement, and he had probably seen enough death on the battlefield to rid him of the taste for violence permanently. Philip Hamilton followed his father's instructions and did not fire at Eacker when the moment came. Eacker, however, fired at Philip; the bullet entered his hip and passed through his right arm.

When Hamilton got word that Philip had been wounded, he rushed to the home of a doctor he knew and fetched him to Angelica Church's home, where he had been taken. Hamilton had always been interested in medicine, and had more than the average layman's understanding of medical matters; when he reached his son's bedside, he immediately took his pulse, and from that moment he seemed to understand that Philip would not live for much longer. Eliza Hamilton, then three months pregnant, appeared at Philip's bedside shortly afterward. When Philip passed away in the early hours of the morning the next day, his mother was lying in the bed with him on one side, and his father on the other.

The *New-York Gazette*, the newspaper which had published Hamilton's first important essay in America, "The Farmer Refuted", printed the following death notice for Philip Hamilton:

"On the morning of the 14th instant, Mr. Philip Hamilton, eldest son of General Hamilton, in the 20th year of his age, of a wound received in a duel with Capt. George I. Eacker. Few events have so much interested the public, whether they consider the youth and promising talents of the deceased, the feelings of most affectionate parents, or the false honor to which his life was sacrificed.

"The duel was occasioned by some frolicksome and satirical expressions made by Mr. Hamilton and a young Mr. Price, at a Theatre, on the Friday preceding, about an oration of Mr. Eacker's and in his hearing. This conduct Mr. Eacker resented in a very intemperate manner, collared Mr. Hamilton, called them damned rascals and villains, and said if he did not hear from them, he would treat them as such. Challenges were consequently sent to him by both.

"Mr. Eacker and Mr. Price met on the Sunday following, and after exchanging four shots without injury to either, the seconds interfered. On Monday, the fatal duel between Mr. Eacker and Mr. Hamilton took place. Young Hamilton was shot through the body, on the first discharge, and fell without firing. He languished until the next morning, and then expired."

After Philip's death, his sister Angelica underwent such a severe emotional breakdown that she never recovered; she had been closest to Philip, and she spent the rest of her life speaking of him as if he was still alive. Hamilton, likewise, entered a profound depression. He lost the remarkably energy that had always characterized his career, and he ceased, for the first time since the war, to write political essays. Only forty-seven years old, his physical appearance altered so much that he seemed to age overnight. He consoled himself that the world could be a very hard place to live in, and trusted that his son was in heaven. While strolling the woods near his house one day with Eliza, Hamilton remarked, "I may have twenty years left, please God, and I will one day build for [my children] a chapel in this grove." The year was 1804; Hamilton had, in fact, only a few months of life left before him.

Vice-President Aaron Burr

Aaron Burr had not enjoyed the confidence of Thomas Jefferson since before their tied election, and Jefferson kept him at a distance during his tenure as vice-president. As a consequence, Burr abandoned hopes of being asked to run on Jefferson's ticket for a second term, and began consolidating support for the upcoming race for governor of New York. Hamilton's only participation in federal government by this time involved writing the occasional political essay and tweaking Jefferson's nose by defending a man who had been charged with writing libelous articles about the president—but he was still active on the local level, and New York politics were still his arena.

Hamilton was just as committed to preventing Burr from becoming New York's governor as he had been committed to keeping him from becoming Vice President. Apart from his personal objections to Burr, Hamilton suspected him of organizing a secessionist movement in secret. Jefferson had recently doubled the size of the nation with the Louisiana Purchase (justifying his actions with a downright Hamiltonian interpretation of the executive powers section of the Constitutional that dismayed many Republicans) and almost all of the states created within the Louisiana Territory were admitted to the union as slave states. This increased the representational voting power of slave interests in Congress to such a degree that some Federalists within the party were whispering privately of allying New Jersey and New York with New England and breaking away from the south. Hamilton, when he caught wind of these rumors, prepared himself to defend the United States against any threat of secession; while Burr, in order to persuade long-time Federalist voters to look past his decades of Republicanism, was encouraging the secession movement by hinting to its proponents that he might be able to further their interests if they were to swing votes his way.

Bad blood had been developing between Hamilton and Burr since the Manhattan Company affair, and the election of 1804 was bringing it to a boil. Exacerbating their discord was a newspaper editor named James Cheetham who printed scandalous articles about Hamilton one week and Burr the next, each article containing insulting quotes that the one had supposedly said about the other. Many people felt that Cheetham was deliberately attempting to provoke some kind of confrontation between Burr and Hamilton. If that was his goal, then he succeeded wildly.

Hamilton threw all his energies into campaigning for the sole opponent challenging Burr for the governorship of New York. His efforts were calculatingly insulting to Burr, because his opponent was not even a Federalist; support for the Federalist party had declined so steeply in New York that during this election the party's only viable candidate was a moderate Republican who could potentially split the party's vote away from Burr. But not even Hamilton could hold a candle to the insults being levied at Burr through the newspapers. Burr was the subject of hateful articles, and curiously, a series of posters that appeared throughout the city bearing various anonymous insinuations of Burrs misdeeds; for reasons that are not entirely clear, Burr was utterly convinced that Hamilton was behind them. Hamilton was used to something close to this level of furious attack in the press, but Burr decidedly was not.

Burr affected not to be bothered by the results of the election, which he lost by over ten thousand votes, but inwardly he was furious with Hamilton, whom he saw, in retrospect, as having been the reason behind his losing the presidency in 1800 as well. Shortly after the gubernatorial race, a letter appeared in a newspaper which had been written by a guest at a private dinner where Hamilton had expressed his bluntest opinions of Burr. In a rush to defend his son-in-law, Philip Schuyler wrote a letter to the same newspaper refuting the story, claiming that Hamilton had never made the statements. In a rush to defend his own honesty, the author of the printed letter claimed that not only had Hamilton said all he was imputed to have said, but there was even more to the story than had been published: "for really, sir, I could detail to you a still more despicable opinion which General Hamilton has expressed of Mr. Burr". That was the final straw; Burr demanded an explanation of Hamilton for the so-called "despicable opinion", and Hamilton responded by quibbling the meaning of the word "despicable". Burr and Hamilton exchanged letters for months, until Burr lost patience and ended the correspondence with a challenge to a duel.

The Duel

In Hamilton's youth, he had adhered rigorously to the dueling codes observed by gentlemen of the late eighteenth century, but his son's death and his renewed interest in religion had left him with a profound distaste for the practice. He concluded that, for his honor's sake, he had no choice but to accept Burr's challenge, but that, for morality's sake, he must do as he had advised

Philip to do the previous year—aim his pistol far afield from Burr and "throw away his fire".

Usually, a challenge was issued no more than a day before the duel took place, but when Hamilton received Burr's challenge, he requested that the duel be put off until after Hamilton had his next appearance before the state Supreme Court, as he did not wish to leave his law clients with unresolved cases if he should happen to be killed. Burr agreed to the delay, and twenty-three days elapsed between the challenge and the duel. Hamilton put this time to useful effect, arranging his papers, writing letters, tending to his finances, naming executors for his estate. One of the letters which he left behind was the "Statement on Impending Duel with Aaron Burr", in which he declares his reasons for accepting Burr's challenge, as well as his intention to avoid any action that might claim Burr's life. An excerpt appears below:

"It is not my design, by what I have said to affix any odium on the conduct of Col Burr, in this case. He doubtless has heard of animadversions of mine which bore very hard upon him; and it is probable that as usual they were accompanied with some falsehoods. He may have supposed himself under a necessity of acting as he has done. I hope the grounds of his proceeding have been such as ought to satisfy his own conscience.

"I trust, at the same time, that the world will do me the Justice to believe, that I have not censured him on light grounds, or from unworthy inducements. I certainly have had strong reasons for what I may have said, though it is possible that in some particulars, I may have been influenced by misconstruction or misinformation. It is also my ardent wish that I may have been more mistaken than I think I have been, and that he by his future conduct may shew himself worthy of all confidence and esteem, and prove an ornament and blessing to his Country.

"As well because it is possible that I may have injured Col Burr, however convinced myself that my opinions and declarations have been well founded, as from my general principles and temper in relation to similar affairs—I have resolved, if our interview is conducted in the usual manner, and it pleases God to give me the opportunity, to reserve and throw away my first fire, and I have thoughts even of reserving my second fire—and thus giving a double opportunity to Col Burr to pause and to reflect."

The duel was set for dawn on July 11th, 1804. Hamilton, having over three weeks to prepare, seems to have lived out his final days in a conscientious way, helping his law clients, spending as much time as possible with his family, hosting dinner parties for his friends, and reflecting on his career and on the future of his country. The duel had to be kept a close secret, otherwise the participants might be arrested before or after their meeting; Hamilton, therefore, could not warn Eliza, though he may not have been inclined to. His letters demonstrate that he was deeply conscious of how much pain his death would bring her, especially so soon after Philip's death. Hamilton seems to have had a deep premonition that this duel, unlike the three he fought in his youth, would actually prove fatal. He had related to Nathan Pendleton, his friend and second, that he meant not to shoot at Burr; Pendleton begged him repeatedly to change his mind, to no avail.

Ron Chernow relates the following anecdote pertaining to Hamilton on the night before the duel took place:

"...he went downstairs and entered a bedroom where a boy was reading a book. This must have been the orphaned boy who had attended the recent outdoor party at the Grange. In an unpublished fragment that may have embroidered the truth, John Church Hamilton reveals that his father entered the room, gazed pensively at the boy, and asked if he would share his bed that night. Hamilton 'soon retired, and placed [the boy's] little hands on his own, he repeated with him the Lord's Prayer.' The child then fell asleep in his arms. This image of Hamilton sleeping with his arms wrapped around an orphaned youth during his last night on earth is inexpressibly poignant and makes one think that his own tormented boyhood weighed on his mind that night."

At dawn on the 11th of July, Hamilton and Burr set out from their respective homes and crossed the river from Manhattan into New Jersey, where dueling was less harshly prosecuted than in New York. The dueling site was a small strip of land that was only visible at low tide—quite close to the spot where Philip Hamilton had fought his duel with George Eacker. Hamilton, as the challenged party, had the right to choose the weapons, and he elected to use the same set of dueling pistols that Philip had borrowed from Angelica Church's husband. He took some considerable time examining the trigger mechanism of the gun and adjusting his glasses before signaling that he was ready for the duel to commence.

Whether Burr or Hamilton shot first has been a matter of historical controversy for 200 years. Martin Van Ness, Burr's second, swore for the rest of his life that Hamilton had fired the first shot, which rang out some twelve feet over Burr's head and lodged in the branch of a nearby tree. Every other witness, however, swore with equal consistency that Burr shot first. His shot tore through Hamilton's side, perforating his liver and lodging in his spine. Hamilton remained conscious, but instantly understood the mortal nature of the wound he had received. He told the surgeon who had accompanied them that he was a dead man; he would live for a few hours yet,

but he was paralyzed from the waist down
already.

The Death of Alexander Hamilton

Hamilton was ferried back across the river and
taken into the home of a wealthy merchant who
lived nearby. Eliza Hamilton was summoned, but
she was told at first only that Hamilton had been
taken ill. The illusion evaporated the moment
she saw him; she had lost her oldest son to a
bullet through the side only a few years before,
and she understood instantly that her husband
had very little time left. Wracked with grief, she
had their seven children brought into the room
so that Hamilton could see them and kiss them
one last time.

Hamilton was in a great deal of pain during the
last hours of his life due to the position of the
bullet in his spine, but his chief source of
agitation was that none of the clergymen who

had come to see him would help him take Communion. Hamilton was known to be very religious as a young man at King's College, where he was witnessed praying on his knees night and day; during the war, however, and during his political career, he had begun to distance himself from religion, feeling that fanaticism of any kind would be dangerous to the new nation. When his political career faltered and his son was killed, his interest in religion was renewed, but he had never been a regular churchgoer, and thus none of his clergyman friends knew him in the character of a parishioner. The fact that he was dying as the result of a duel increased their reluctance to administer last rites, since he would have no opportunity to demonstrate repentance. At last, Benjamin Moore, an Episcopal bishop, agreed to give him Communion on the condition that he promise to renounce dueling if he should live. Hamilton gladly agreed to do so.

When Hamilton passed away on the afternoon of July 12, 1804, at the age of forty-nine, it was in a room crowded to capacity with friends and family members who had come to pray or merely sit in his presence. His last words, or very nearly, were in reference to the secession crisis amongst the northern Federalists: "if they break this union, they will break my heart." When Eliza Hamilton returned home, she came upon the short, lovely letter that Hamilton left for her amongst his papers: "The consolations of religion, my beloved, can alone support you and these you have a right to enjoy. Fly to the bosom of your God and be comforted. With my last idea, I shall cherish the sweet hope of meeting you in a better world. Adieu best of wives and best of women. Embrace all my darling children for me."

Hamilton's death sent shockwaves through New York, and through the country at large, which united in mourning him, though it had never united in approving of him. It was said that not even George Washington had so solemn a funeral, attended by so many mourners. Men, women, and children lined the streets to watch the procession go by. Hamilton's eulogy was written and delivered by his long-time friend and fellow abolitionist, Governeur Morris, who struggled somewhat to encapsulate Hamilton's legacy in words. The final paragraph of his speech, however, sounds like it was written by someone who knew him:

"You have long witnessed his professional conduct, and felt his unrivalled eloquence. You know how well he performed the duties of a Citizen—you know that he never courted your favour by adulation, or the sacrifice of his own judgment. You have seen him contending against you, and saving your dearest interests, as it were, in spite of yourselves. And you now feel and enjoy the benefits resulting from the firm energy of his conduct. Bear this testimony to the memory of my departed friend. I charge you to protect his fame—It is all he has left—all that these poor orphan children will inherit from their father. But, my countrymen, that Fame may be a rich treasure to you also. Let it be the test by which to examine those who solicit your favour."

Hamilton's premature death left his family saddled with debts that his estate could not pay. But in testament to their admiration for one of the greatest men of the revolutionary generation, his friends took up a subscription—not unlike the subscription that sent Hamilton to America from St. Croix as a boy in the first place. They gathered eighty thousand dollars in a fund that was to support Eliza and her children for the rest of her life. Eliza Hamilton lived another fifty years, until the very eve of the Civil War. Everything that is known about Hamilton today is owed to her careful preservation of his papers throughout her lifetime.

Other books available by Michael W. Simmons on Kindle, paperback and audio:

Nikola Tesla: Prophet Of The Modern
Technological Age

Albert Einstein: Father Of the Modern Scientific
Age

Further Reading

Alexander Hamilton, by Ron Chernow

Letter from Alexander Hamilton to William Jackson, August 1800

http://founders.archives.gov/documents/ Hamilton/01-25-02-0068

From Alexander Hamilton to the Royal Danish American Gazette, 6 September 1772

http://founders.archives.gov/documents/ Hamilton/01-01-02-0042

"A Full Vindication of the Measures of Congress"

http://founders.archives.gov/documents/ Hamilton/01-01-02-0054

"The Farmer Refuted"

http://founders.archives.gov/documents/ Hamilton/01-01-02-0057

Letter from Alexander Hamilton to George Washington, before 29 January 1778

http://founders.archives.gov/?q=Author%3A%22Hamilton%2C%20Alexander%22%20Period%3A%22Revolutionary%20War%22&s=1111311111&r=113

Letter from Alexander Hamilton to Elizabeth Schuyler, 20 July 1780

http://founders.archives.gov/?q=Author%3A%22Hamilton%2C%20Alexander%22%20Period%3A%22Revolutionary%20War%22%20Recipient%3A%22Schuyler%2C%20Elizabeth%22&s=1111311111&r=7

The Federalist Papers, No. 1, by Alexander Hamilton

http://www.constitution.org/fed/federa01.htm

Report on Public Credit

http://www.wwnorton.com/college/history/archive/resources/documents/ch08_02.htm

Opinion as to the Constitutionality of the Bank of the United States

http://www.constitution.org/mon/ah-bank.htm

The Reynolds Pamphlet

http://founders.archives.gov/documents/Hamilton/01-21-02-0138-0002

Washington's Farewell Address

http://avalon.law.yale.edu/18th_century/washing.asp

Letter from Alexander Hamilton Concerning the Public Conduct and Character of John Adams, Esq., President of the United States

http://founders.archives.gov/documents/Hamilton/01-25-02-0110-0002

Death of Philip Hamilton

https://itshamiltime.com/2015/03/17/the-death-of-philip-hamilton/

Statement on Impending Duel with Aaron Burr

http://founders.archives.gov/documents/
Hamilton/01-26-02-0001-0241

Eulogy on the Death of Alexander Hamilton, by
Governeur Morris

https://itshamiltime.com/2015/07/12/go
uverneur-morriss-eulogy-of-alexander-
hamilton/